Home Buying Made Easy in Malta

A Beginner's Guide to Property Investment

Alistair McLeod

Copyright © 2024 Alistair McLeod

All rights reserved.

ISBN: 9798334292147

DISCLAIMER

The information provided in this book is for general informational purposes only. While every effort has been made to ensure the accuracy and reliability of the content, the author and publisher make no representations or warranties of any kind, express or implied, about the completeness, accuracy, reliability, suitability, or availability concerning the book or the information, products, services, or related graphics contained in the book for any purpose. Any reliance you place on such information is strictly at your own risk.

The author and publisher shall not be held liable or responsible for any errors, omissions, or inaccuracies, nor for any actions taken based on the information provided within this book. Always consult with a professional or expert in the relevant field before making any decisions based on the content of this book.

HOME BUYING MADE EASY IN MALTA

CONTENTS

Disclaimer iii

Contents v

Introduction x

Chapter 1: Understanding the Maltese Real Estate Landscape 1

   1.1: The Unique Appeal of Malta's Real Estate 2

   1.2: Key Regions and Their Property Profiles 5

   1.3: Historical Trends and Current Market Dynamics 8

   1.4: Types of Properties Available in Malta 11

   1.5: Malta's Real Estate: A Comparative Global Perspective . 14

Chapter 2: The Initial Steps in Property Investment 17

   2.1: Assessing Your Investment Goals and Budget 18

   2.2: The Importance of Research and Due Diligence 21

   2.3: Building a Reliable Property Investment Team 24

   2.4: The Role of Real Estate Agents in Malta 28

   2.5: Understanding the Maltese Property Investment Language 32

Chapter 3: Financial Considerations in Property Investment . 36

   3.1: Understanding Taxes and Fees in Malta's Real Estate 37

   3.2: Financing Options for Property Investment 41

   3.3: The Impact of Interest Rates on Property Investments .. 45

   3.4: Budgeting for Additional Costs 49

   3.5: Investment Strategies for Maximum Returns 53

Chapter 4: Legal Framework and Compliance 57

4.1: Navigating Malta's Property Laws 58

4.2: The Role of Legal Counsel in Property Transactions........62

4.3: Understanding Contracts and Agreements 66

4.4: Property Rights and Ownership Regulations 70

4.5: Resolving Legal Disputes in Real Estate Transactions.....74

Chapter 5: The Buying Process in Detail 78

5.1: Searching for the Right Property 79

5.2: Making an Offer and Negotiating Terms 83

5.3: The Promise of Sale Agreement (Konvenju) 86

5.4: Due Diligence and Property Inspection 89

5.5: Finalizing the Sale: The Act of Completion 93

Chapter 6: Renting vs. Buying in Malta 96

6.1: Pros and Cons of Buying vs. Renting................................97

6.2: Long-term Investment Potential of Buying....................101

6.3: Flexibility and Ease of Renting 105

6.4: Understanding Rental Laws and Regulations 109

6.5: Making the Decision: Rent or Buy?................................112

Chapter 7: Special Considerations for Foreign Investors.......116

7.1: Restrictions and Opportunities for Non-Residents........117

7.2: Navigating the Acquisition of Immovable Property (AIP) Permit 121

7.3: Currency and Exchange Rate Considerations 124

7.4: Residency and Visa Implications of Property Investment 128

7.5: Cultural and Social Adaptation for Foreign Investors ...132

Chapter 8: Maximizing Property Value ...136

8.1: Renovation and Remodeling: Enhancing Property Value ...137

8.2: The Importance of Location and Amenities ...141

8.3: Current Trends in Maltese Property Design ...144

8.4: Sustainable and Eco-Friendly Property Investments ...148

8.5: Marketing Your Property Effectively ...152

Chapter 9: The Role of Technology in Real Estate ...156

9.1: Online Platforms and Digital Tools for Property Search ...157

9.2: The Impact of Virtual Reality in Real Estate Viewing ...161

9.3: Utilizing Big Data for Market Analysis ...165

9.4: The Role of Social Media in Real Estate Marketing ...169

9.5: Future Trends in Real Estate Technology ...173

Chapter 10: Risk Management in Property Investment ...177

10.1: Identifying and Mitigating Risks in Real Estate ...178

10.2: The Importance of Insurance in Property Investment 182

10.3: Economic Factors Affecting Real Estate Markets ...186

10.4: Political and Regulatory Changes and Their Impact ...190

10.5: Building a Diverse Real Estate Portfolio ...194

Chapter 11: Post-Purchase Considerations ...198

11.1: Property Management Essentials ...199

11.2: Understanding Maintenance and Upkeep Responsibilities ...203

11.3: Engaging with the Community and Neighbors 207

11.4: Dealing with Tenants and Rental Agreements............211

11.5: Long-term Strategic Planning for Property Owners....215

Chapter 12: Future Prospects in Maltese Real Estate 219

12.1: Predicting Market Trends and Their Impact...............220

12.2: Opportunities in Commercial vs. Residential Real Estate 224

12.3: The Role of Government Policies in Shaping the Market 227

12.4: International Perspectives on Maltese Real Estate 231

12.5: Preparing for the Future as a Property Investor in Malta 235

Conclusion..239

Your Voice Matters..242

About the Author 244

INTRODUCTION

Welcome to "Home Buying Made Easy in Malta: A Beginner's Guide to Property Investment." As a seasoned author and expert in the realm of property investment and marketing, I understand the importance of practical, actionable information. In this guide, you won't find pages filled with glossy photos or basic country details such as Malta's population, currency, or official language. I assume that if you've picked up this book, you've already acquainted yourself with these fundamental aspects.

What I offer you here is something far more valuable: a distillation of facts, a pure know-how derived from years of experience and thorough research. This book is designed to equip you with the essential knowledge and tools required to navigate Malta's unique real estate market confidently. Whether you're a first-time homebuyer, a seasoned investor, or simply exploring the possibility of owning property in Malta, this guide will serve as your roadmap, illuminating the path through the complexities of real estate transactions, legal intricacies, and market dynamics in Malta. Let's embark on this journey together, towards making informed and successful property investments in this beautiful Mediterranean haven.

CHAPTER 1: UNDERSTANDING THE MALTESE REAL ESTATE LANDSCAPE

Embarking on a journey into the Maltese real estate market is akin to discovering a hidden gem in the heart of the Mediterranean. This chapter is designed to lay the foundation for your property investment venture in Malta. It delves into the unique allure of Malta's real estate, offering insights into the diverse regions and their distinct property characteristics. We'll explore the historical trends shaping the current market, the types of properties available, and how Malta's real estate stands in a global context. This chapter aims to provide you with a comprehensive understanding of the landscape, ensuring you're well-equipped to make informed decisions in this dynamic market.

1.1: THE UNIQUE APPEAL OF MALTA'S REAL ESTATE

Malta, a small archipelago in the heart of the Mediterranean, offers an intriguing real estate market that stands out for several reasons. The island's real estate has a unique appeal, driven by its rich history, strategic location, and vibrant culture. This section explores these aspects, highlighting what makes Maltese property an attractive investment.

Historical Significance

Malta's history is deeply woven into the fabric of its buildings and architecture. From ancient temples to baroque palaces, the island is a living museum, offering properties that are not just homes but pieces of history. This historical significance adds a unique charm to Maltese properties, attracting investors and homeowners who seek a connection to the past.

Strategic Location

Malta's position in the Mediterranean has historically made it a strategic hub for trade and military operations. Today, this translates into a bustling economy and a cosmopolitan lifestyle that appeals to investors and expatriates. The island's location also means that it enjoys more than 300 days of sunshine a year, making it an ideal destination for those seeking a warm climate.

Cultural Richness

Maltese culture is a tapestry of influences, from the Phoenicians and Romans to the Knights of St. John. This cultural richness is reflected in its real estate, where one can find a blend of architectural styles. The island's calendar is filled with festivals, arts, and culinary experiences, adding to the lifestyle appeal of owning property here.

Stable Economy and Political Climate

Malta boasts a stable economy and political environment, which is reassuring for property investors. The country's membership in the European Union and the Eurozone adds an extra layer of economic stability and ease of doing business. This stability is a significant factor for those looking to invest in real estate, as it promises a lower risk and potential for steady appreciation.

Attractive Residency Programs

Malta offers several residency and citizenship programs that are attractive to foreign investors. These programs often include benefits like tax incentives and ease of travel within the Schengen Area. The accessibility of these programs makes Malta an appealing destination for non-EU investors looking for a foothold in Europe.

Diverse Real Estate Portfolio

The Maltese real estate market offers a wide range of properties, from traditional townhouses and farmhouses to modern apartments and luxury villas. This diversity means that there is something to suit every taste and budget. The island's compact size also means that properties are never far from the sea, adding to their appeal.

Strong Rental Market

Malta's strong rental market is driven by its growing expatriate community and thriving tourism industry. This creates opportunities for investors to generate income through short-term holiday lets or long-term rentals. The demand for rental properties is bolstered by the island's appeal as a retirement destination and its growing status as a hub for industries like gaming and blockchain.

Quality of Life

Living in Malta offers a high quality of life, with excellent healthcare, a safe environment, and a friendly, English-speaking community. The Mediterranean lifestyle, characterized by a relaxed pace and outdoor living, is another draw for those looking to invest in Maltese property.

Government Initiatives in Real Estate

The Maltese government has implemented various initiatives to encourage investment in the real estate sector. These include favorable tax rates, schemes for first-time buyers, and incentives for property development. Such initiatives not only boost the real estate market but also make it more accessible for both local and foreign investors.

The appeal of Malta's real estate market lies in its unique blend of historical charm, strategic location, cultural richness, and a stable and welcoming environment for investors. Whether one is drawn to the island's rich history, its sunny Mediterranean lifestyle, or the potential for a sound investment, Malta's real estate market offers opportunities that are hard to find elsewhere. With its diverse range of properties, strong rental demand, and favorable investment climate, Malta stands out as a top choice for those looking to invest in real estate in the Mediterranean.

1.2: KEY REGIONS AND THEIR PROPERTY PROFILES

Malta, though small in size, is richly diverse in its regional real estate offerings. Each area of this charming archipelago presents unique characteristics, appealing to a wide array of preferences and needs. This section will delve into the key regions of Malta and their distinct property profiles, offering insights for potential investors and homebuyers.

Valletta: The Capital's Charm

Valletta, the capital city of Malta, is a UNESCO World Heritage site known for its historical and cultural significance. The real estate here is characterized by beautifully preserved baroque architecture, narrow streets, and grand townhouses. These properties often feature traditional Maltese balconies and intricate facades. Investing in Valletta is ideal for those who appreciate historical architecture and wish to be at the heart of Malta's cultural scene.

Sliema and St. Julian's: Modern and Cosmopolitan

Sliema and the adjacent town of St. Julian's are the epitome of modern Maltese living. These areas are known for their bustling urban atmosphere, with a plethora of shops, restaurants, and entertainment options. The real estate market here is dominated by contemporary apartments, penthouses, and luxury developments. These properties offer modern amenities and are favored by young professionals and those seeking a vibrant lifestyle.

The Three Cities: Historical and Upcoming

The Three Cities - Vittoriosa, Senglea, and Cospicua - are gaining popularity for their authentic charm and maritime history. This area offers a mix of traditional Maltese houses and newly developed properties. With ongoing restoration and development projects, the Three Cities are becoming a sought-after location for those looking for a blend of history and modern living.

Mdina and Rabat: Timeless Elegance

Mdina, the old capital, and its neighboring town Rabat are known for their timeless elegance. Mdina, a fortified city, is famous for its medieval and baroque architecture. Properties here are limited but highly coveted, offering a serene and aristocratic living experience. Rabat, while more accessible, still maintains a historic charm with its mix of old townhouses and modern residences.

The Northern Region: Family-Friendly and Scenic

The Northern part of Malta, including areas like Mellieha and St. Paul's Bay, is known for its scenic landscapes and family-friendly atmosphere. Properties in this region range from traditional farmhouses to modern family homes, many with stunning sea views. This region is ideal for those seeking a quieter lifestyle, close to some of Malta's best beaches and natural attractions.

Gozo: Rustic Charm and Tranquility

Gozo, Malta's sister island, offers a more laid-back, rustic lifestyle. The real estate here includes traditional farmhouses, often with features like limestone walls, wood beams, and large courtyards. Gozo is ideal for those looking for a tranquil retreat or a slower pace of life, surrounded by unspoiled natural beauty.

The South: Untapped Potential

Southern Malta is often considered an untapped gem in the real estate market. This region offers affordable property options, including traditional townhouses and villas. The South is known for its quieter villages, local traditions, and beautiful coastline, making it an attractive option for those seeking a more authentic Maltese experience.

Central Malta: The Heart of the Island

Central Malta, encompassing towns like Birkirkara, Balzan, and Attard, offers a balance of urban and suburban living. The real estate here ranges from modern apartments to traditional Maltese houses and villas. Central Malta is well-connected and convenient, ideal for families and individuals who want to be at the center of everything but still enjoy a sense of community.

Luxury Developments: Exclusive Living

Malta has seen a rise in luxury developments, such as Portomaso in St. Julian's and Tigne Point in Sliema. These high-end residential areas offer luxury apartments, penthouses, and amenities like swimming pools, fitness centers, and shopping complexes. These developments cater to the upper market segment, offering exclusivity and high-end living.

Investment Opportunities Across the Island

The diverse regions of Malta each present unique investment opportunities. From the historical allure of Valletta and the Three Cities to the modern appeal of Sliema and St. Julian's, and the rustic charm of Gozo, there is something for every investor and homebuyer. The key to successful investment lies in understanding the distinct character and potential of each region, aligning it with one's investment goals and lifestyle preferences.

The Maltese property market, with its rich variety of regions and property types, offers a wealth of opportunities for those looking to invest in real estate. Whether one is drawn to the urban excitement of the central localities, the historical depth of the cities, the rustic appeal of Gozo, or the emerging potential of the South, Malta's real estate landscape is as diverse as it is compelling.

1.3: HISTORICAL TRENDS AND CURRENT MARKET DYNAMICS

Malta's real estate market is a fascinating blend of historical trends and contemporary dynamics. Understanding these elements is crucial for anyone looking to invest or buy property in Malta. This section delves into the historical trends that have shaped the Maltese property market and examines the current dynamics at play.

A Look into the Past

Historically, Malta's real estate market has been influenced by its strategic location in the Mediterranean. This has brought a constant influx of foreign influences and investments, shaping the property landscape. Post-World War II, Malta saw a significant reconstruction phase, leading to the development of new housing areas and the modernization of old ones. The joining of the European Union in 2004 marked another pivotal moment, opening up the market to broader European investment and leading to a surge in property development and prices.

Boom of the Early 21st Century

The early 2000s witnessed a significant boom in Malta's real estate sector. Fueled by economic growth, low-interest rates, and favorable lending conditions, there was a marked increase in property development. This period saw the rise of luxury developments and high-rise buildings, transforming the skyline in areas like Sliema and St. Julian's. Demand was high, both from local buyers and a growing number of foreign investors, driven by Malta's appealing residency programs and stable economy.

Global Financial Crisis and Its Aftermath

The global financial crisis of 2008 had a relatively muted impact on Malta compared to other countries. While there was a slowdown in the market, the effects were not as severe, and the market quickly rebounded. This resilience was due to Malta's conservative banking practices and the continued demand for property, particularly from foreign buyers looking for a safe investment haven.

Current Market Dynamics

As of 2024, the Maltese real estate market is characterized by a mix of steady growth and evolving trends. The demand for property remains strong, driven by factors such as Malta's growing reputation as a business hub, its lifestyle appeal, and ongoing foreign investment. However, there's a noticeable shift towards more sustainable and community-focused developments, reflecting a broader global trend towards responsible living.

The Rise of Sustainable Developments

Sustainability has become a key factor in current property developments. There is an increasing demand for energy-efficient homes, green spaces, and developments that blend with the natural environment. This shift is not just driven by environmental concerns but also by the understanding that sustainable properties hold their value better and offer a higher quality of living.

Impact of Technology and Remote Work

The recent global shift towards remote work has also impacted Malta's real estate market. There's a growing demand for properties that can accommodate home offices and high-tech amenities. This trend is attracting a new demographic of buyers who are looking for a balance between work and the idyllic Maltese lifestyle.

Changing Demographics and Buyer Preferences

The demographic profile of property buyers in Malta is evolving. There's an increase in younger buyers and foreign residents who bring different expectations and preferences. This shift is leading to a diversification in the types of properties being developed, with a focus on modern amenities, connectivity, and lifestyle-oriented features.

Affordability and Housing Concerns

Affordability remains a concern in the Maltese property market, particularly for first-time buyers and the younger population. The government and private developers are addressing this through various initiatives, including affordable housing schemes and incentives for first-time buyers.

Foreign Investment and Market Stability

Foreign investment continues to play a significant role in Malta's property market. The stability of Malta's economy, its strategic location, and attractive residency programs make it an appealing destination for international investors. This influx of foreign capital has been instrumental in driving development and maintaining market stability.

Regional Variations

There are notable regional variations in Malta's property market. Areas like Valletta and the Central region continue to see high demand and price appreciation, while other areas, particularly in the South and Gozo, offer more affordable options with potential for growth.

Future Outlook

The Maltese real estate market shows signs of continuing its positive trajectory, with ongoing developments, foreign investment, and a focus on sustainability and modern living. The market's resilience, diverse property offerings, and appeal to a broad spectrum of buyers suggest a robust future for Malta's real estate sector. The understanding of historical trends and current dynamics is key to navigating this vibrant market, providing insights for successful investment and property ownership in Malta.

1.4: TYPES OF PROPERTIES AVAILABLE IN MALTA

The Maltese archipelago, though small, offers a remarkably diverse range of property types, catering to various lifestyles and investment preferences. This rich diversity in real estate is a reflection of Malta's multifaceted culture and history. This section explores the various types of properties available in Malta, providing insights into each to help potential buyers and investors make informed decisions.

Traditional Maltese Townhouses

One of the most charming and sought-after property types in Malta is the traditional Maltese townhouse. These houses are renowned for their distinct architectural features, such as patterned tiles, wooden balconies, and intricately designed facades. Located primarily in urban areas and older towns, these townhouses offer a glimpse into the Maltese way of life and are a popular choice for those seeking a property with character and history.

Apartments and Penthouses

Apartments are the most common type of property in Malta's urban areas, especially in towns like Sliema, St. Julian's, and Valletta. Ranging from modest studios to luxurious penthouses, apartments in Malta cater to a wide range of budgets and preferences. Modern apartments often come with amenities like pools, gyms, and underground parking, making them a convenient option for both residents and investors.

Villas and Detached Houses

For those seeking more space and privacy, villas and detached houses are an ideal choice. These properties are typically found in more suburban areas or on the outskirts of towns. They often feature spacious layouts, gardens, and swimming pools, offering a more relaxed and luxurious lifestyle. Villas in Malta are particularly popular among families and expatriates.

Farmhouses and Country Homes

The rural areas of Malta and Gozo are dotted with traditional farmhouses and country homes. These properties are characterized by their rustic charm, with features like stone walls, wooden beams, and large courtyards. Farmhouses are particularly popular in Gozo, where they are often used as holiday homes or rentals, providing a tranquil escape from the hustle and bustle of urban life.

Luxury Developments and Lifestyle Projects

Malta has seen a rise in luxury developments and lifestyle projects in recent years. These high-end developments, such as Portomaso in St. Julian's and Tigne Point in Sliema, offer a range of luxury apartments and penthouses. These projects are designed to provide a comprehensive lifestyle experience with facilities like marinas, shopping centers, and leisure amenities, catering to the upper market segment.

Historical Palazzos and Unique Properties

For those interested in owning a piece of Malta's history, there are historical palazzos and unique properties available. These grand buildings, often dating back centuries, offer a unique living experience. They are usually located in the older parts of towns and cities and are prized for their architectural beauty and historical significance.

Commercial Real Estate

In addition to residential properties, Malta offers a variety of commercial real estate options. These include office spaces, retail outlets, and hospitality properties. The commercial real estate market in Malta has been growing steadily, driven by the island's economic development and its status as an international business hub.

Development Opportunities

For investors and developers, Malta offers opportunities in property development. The government's supportive policies and incentives for development have led to a growth in projects ranging from small-scale renovations to large mixed-use developments.

A Place for Everyone

The diversity in Malta's property market means that there is something for everyone, whether one is looking for a cozy apartment in a bustling town, a luxurious villa with sea views, a rustic farmhouse in the countryside, or an investment in commercial real estate. This variety allows buyers and investors to find properties that not only meet their needs and preferences but also offer potential for appreciation and return on investment.

The Maltese real estate landscape, with its array of property types, reflects the rich tapestry of the island's culture and history. Understanding these property types is crucial for anyone considering investing in or moving to Malta. Each type offers its own unique set of benefits and considerations, catering to the diverse needs of the local and international community in Malta.

1.5: MALTA'S REAL ESTATE: A COMPARATIVE GLOBAL PERSPECTIVE

When considering Malta's real estate market, it's insightful to place it within a global context. This comparative analysis not only highlights the uniqueness of Maltese property but also provides a broader understanding of its position in the international real estate landscape.

Malta vs. Mediterranean Counterparts

Malta often draws comparisons with other Mediterranean destinations such as Spain, Italy, and Greece. However, Malta's market has distinct advantages, such as its robust legal system and stable political climate, which offer security to investors. Additionally, Malta's status as an English-speaking member of the European Union adds a layer of accessibility for international investors.

Property Value and Appreciation

In comparison to major European capitals, property in Malta is generally more affordable, yet it has shown consistent appreciation over the years. This steady growth makes Malta an attractive option for those looking to invest in property with a potential for good return on investment.

Rental Yields and Market Stability

Rental yields in Malta are competitive when compared to other European markets. The high demand for rentals, driven by tourism and a growing expatriate community, contributes to this. Furthermore, Malta's real estate market has demonstrated resilience during economic fluctuations, showing less volatility than many other European markets.

Sustainability and Development Trends

Globally, there is a growing emphasis on sustainability in real estate. Malta is aligning with this trend, increasingly focusing on eco-friendly and sustainable development. This approach not only addresses environmental concerns but also caters to a growing segment of environmentally conscious investors and residents.

Government Policies and Incentives

Malta's government offers various incentives and residency programs that are particularly attractive to foreign investors, more so than many other countries. These programs, combined with favorable tax conditions, make Malta stand out as a destination for real estate investment.

Ease of Doing Business

The ease of doing business in Malta, including in the real estate sector, is comparatively high. Procedures for buying property are straightforward, and there is a well-established legal framework protecting property rights. This ease attracts investors who might be deterred by more complex or less transparent systems in other countries.

Tourism Impact on Real Estate

The impact of tourism on Malta's real estate market is significant and more pronounced than in many larger countries. The steady flow of tourists year-round fuels demand for short-term rentals, boosting the property market and providing opportunities for investors in holiday rentals.

Expatriate and Retirement Appeal

Malta is increasingly popular as a destination for expatriates and retirees, particularly from other European countries and the UK. The combination of a mild climate, English as an official language, and a high quality of life makes it an appealing choice. This demographic contributes to a diverse and dynamic property market.

Luxury and High-End Segment

The luxury property segment in Malta, including high-end apartments, villas, and lifestyle developments, is growing and compares favorably with luxury markets in other popular destinations. These properties offer a blend of modern amenities and unique Maltese character, attracting a discerning international clientele.

Regional Diversity and Investment Potential

Unlike many small island nations, Malta offers a surprising regional diversity in its real estate market. Each region has its unique appeal and investment potential, from the historic properties in Valletta and the Three Cities to the modern developments in Sliema and St. Julian's, and the rustic charm of properties in Gozo.

Global Interest and Market Dynamics

The global interest in Malta's real estate has led to a dynamic market that balances traditional Maltese characteristics with modern demands and trends. This balance is unique and contributes to the market's appeal to a broad range of international buyers and investors.

The comparative global perspective of Malta's real estate market reveals a unique combination of stability, growth potential, and appeal to a diverse range of buyers and investors. Its position within the broader European and Mediterranean context highlights its strengths and opportunities, making it a compelling choice for those looking to invest in international real estate. The island's unique characteristics, combined with its strategic location, stable economy, and appealing lifestyle, position Malta's real estate market as both distinct and desirable in the global arena.

CHAPTER 2:
THE INITIAL STEPS IN PROPERTY INVESTMENT

Embarking on property investment in Malta is an exciting journey, one that begins with a solid understanding of the initial steps involved. This chapter is crafted to guide you through these crucial early stages, ensuring a strong foundation for your investment endeavors. We will explore how to align your investment goals with your budget, the significance of thorough research, the importance of assembling a reliable team, and the role of real estate agents in Malta. Additionally, we'll delve into the nuances of the Maltese property investment language, equipping you with the necessary knowledge to navigate this market confidently. These initial steps are pivotal in setting the stage for a successful property investment journey in Malta.

2.1: ASSESSING YOUR INVESTMENT GOALS AND BUDGET

When venturing into the realm of property investment, the first and perhaps most critical step is to clearly define your investment goals and assess your budget. This process is not merely about numbers; it's about understanding your aspirations, risk tolerance, and long-term objectives. This section will guide you through the key considerations in aligning your goals with your financial capabilities to make informed investment decisions in Malta's real estate market.

Understanding Your Investment Goals

Investment goals can vary widely among individuals. Some may seek long-term capital growth, while others might prioritize immediate rental yields. Your goals could be driven by a desire for a retirement home, a vacation property, or a diversification of assets. It's important to articulate what you hope to achieve with your investment. This clarity will influence your decision-making process, from the type of property you select to the location.

Risk Tolerance and Investment Horizon

Your risk tolerance and investment horizon are integral to shaping your investment strategy. If you have a high risk tolerance and a long-term horizon, you might consider properties with higher potential for capital appreciation, which may also come with more volatility. Conversely, if you prefer stability and have a shorter investment horizon, properties with steady rental income and lower risk may be more suitable.

Budget Assessment and Financial Planning

Determining your budget is a critical step. This involves not only assessing your current financial resources but also understanding your borrowing capacity if you're considering a mortgage. It's crucial to account for all the costs associated with property investment, including purchase costs, taxes, ongoing maintenance, and potential renovation expenses. A well-thought-out budget will prevent overextension and ensure your investment remains sustainable.

Market Research and Realistic Expectations

Conducting thorough market research is indispensable. Understanding the property market trends, prices in different regions of Malta, and the potential for growth or rental yield will help in setting realistic expectations. It's important to align your budget with the market realities, acknowledging that certain areas or property types may be out of reach or not in line with your investment goals.

The Importance of Liquidity

Considering the liquidity of your investment is important. Real estate is typically a less liquid asset class compared to stocks or bonds. You should consider how quickly you might need to convert your property investment into cash and how that aligns with market conditions.

Incorporating Professional Advice

Seeking advice from financial advisors, real estate experts, and legal professionals can provide valuable insights into your financial planning. These professionals can help assess the feasibility of your budget and investment goals, ensuring that your strategy is sound and in line with market conditions.

Diversification Strategies

If you're an experienced investor, diversifying your real estate portfolio can spread risk. This might involve investing in different types of properties, such as residential, commercial, or rental properties, or investing in different regions within Malta or abroad.

Tax Considerations and Implications

Understanding the tax implications of property investment is crucial. Different types of properties and investment strategies may have varying tax liabilities. It's advisable to consult with a tax professional to understand these implications and how they affect your overall investment strategy and returns.

Adjusting Goals and Budget Over Time

Your investment goals and budget are not static; they may evolve over time based on personal circumstances, market conditions, and other factors. Regularly reviewing and adjusting your investment strategy is a prudent practice to ensure it continues to align with your goals and the changing market landscape.

Long-Term Perspective

Property investment is often most successful when approached with a long-term perspective. Real estate markets can fluctuate, and having the patience to ride out market cycles can be beneficial. A long-term view allows you to leverage the potential for capital appreciation and build wealth over time.

Personal Considerations

Finally, personal considerations such as family needs, lifestyle preferences, and retirement plans should also factor into your decision. Your investment should complement your personal life goals and not just financial objectives.

In assessing your investment goals and budget for property investment in Malta, a comprehensive and thoughtful approach is key. This involves understanding your personal and financial objectives, conducting thorough market research, seeking professional advice, and being prepared to adjust your strategy as needed. With a well-defined plan, you're better positioned to make informed decisions and navigate the Maltese real estate market effectively.

2.2: THE IMPORTANCE OF RESEARCH AND DUE DILIGENCE

In the journey of property investment, research and due diligence are the cornerstones that can either make or break your investment. This detailed exploration into the significance of research and due diligence in the Maltese real estate market provides a comprehensive guide to understanding the market, assessing potential risks, and making well-informed decisions.

Market Research: Understanding the Maltese Real Estate Landscape

The first step in your due diligence process should be to gain a thorough understanding of the Maltese real estate landscape. This involves studying market trends, pricing, and future projections. Investigate factors such as property demand in different areas, historical price trends, and potential future developments that could affect property values. Such information is crucial in identifying areas with growth potential and avoiding overvalued markets.

Legal Research: Navigating Malta's Property Laws

Understanding the legal framework surrounding property transactions in Malta is vital. This includes knowledge about property rights, transfer processes, and any legal restrictions, especially for foreign investors. It's advisable to familiarize yourself with the Acquisition of Immovable Property (AIP) permit process, if applicable. Legal due diligence helps in avoiding legal pitfalls that could result in costly delays or legal disputes.

Financial Due Diligence: Assessing Costs and Returns

Financial due diligence entails a thorough analysis of the costs involved in the property transaction and the expected returns. This includes not just the purchase price, but also additional costs such as taxes, legal fees, stamp duty, and ongoing maintenance costs. Analyzing potential rental yields or capital appreciation is crucial in evaluating the investment's profitability.

Technical Due Diligence: Property Inspection and Valuation

Inspecting the property and getting a professional valuation is an essential part of due diligence. This process helps in identifying any structural issues, necessary repairs, or renovations that might affect the property's value or lead to future expenditures. A professional valuation also ensures that you pay a fair price for the property.

Location Analysis: The Key to Successful Investment

The location of a property is one of the most critical factors in real estate investment. Research the area's infrastructure, accessibility, future development plans, and neighborhood demographics. Factors like proximity to amenities, schools, public transport, and commercial areas can significantly impact property value and rental potential.

Understanding the Rental Market

If your investment goal is to generate rental income, understanding the rental market dynamics is crucial. Research rental rates, occupancy levels, and tenant demand in the area. This knowledge is vital in assessing the property's potential for generating steady rental income and its appeal to potential tenants.

Risks Assessment: Identifying Potential Pitfalls

Identifying and assessing potential risks is a fundamental aspect of due diligence. This includes market risks, such as economic downturns, changes in government policies affecting property ownership, and environmental risks like flooding or erosion. Being aware of these risks helps in developing strategies to mitigate them.

Seeking Professional Advice

While individual research is invaluable, consulting with real estate professionals, legal advisors, and financial experts in Malta can provide deeper insights and help validate your findings. These professionals can offer specialized knowledge, local expertise, and advice tailored to your specific investment scenario.

Long-Term Perspective in Research

Property investment is typically a long-term endeavor, and your research should take a long-term perspective. Consider how the property and its location might evolve over the years and how global and local economic conditions might impact the real estate market.

Cultural and Social Research

Understanding the local culture and social dynamics of the area where you're investing is also important. This includes learning about the lifestyle, community, and social norms, which can affect the property's appeal to future buyers or renters.

Keeping Up with Regulations and Policies

Staying informed about changes in regulations, tax laws, and government policies affecting real estate is essential. These can have significant implications on your investment, and staying updated can help in making proactive adjustments to your investment strategy.

In sum, research and due diligence are fundamental processes that underpin successful property investment in Malta. They involve a multifaceted approach, encompassing market analysis, legal and financial scrutiny, property inspection, and understanding the local context. Thorough due diligence not only helps in making informed investment decisions but also in mitigating risks and maximizing the potential for a successful investment.

2.3: BUILDING A RELIABLE PROPERTY INVESTMENT TEAM

Successful property investment in Malta, or anywhere for that matter, often hinges on the strength and reliability of your investment team. This team is a coalition of professionals who guide and support you through the intricacies of real estate investment. This section focuses on identifying and assembling a team of experts that can contribute significantly to the success of your property investment journey.

Real Estate Agent: Your Primary Guide

A proficient real estate agent is an invaluable member of your team. They offer deep insights into the local market, help in finding properties that match your investment criteria, and assist in negotiation processes. An agent with a strong track record in the Maltese market can provide insider knowledge on property trends, pricing, and areas with potential for growth.

Legal Advisor: Safeguarding Your Interests

The complexities of property law necessitate having a skilled legal advisor. This professional ensures that all legal aspects of your property transactions are handled correctly, from contracts to compliance with local laws and regulations. They play a crucial role in safeguarding your interests, particularly in areas such as title searches, property rights, and transaction legality.

Financial Advisor: Managing Your Investment Portfolio

A financial advisor helps in aligning your property investment with your overall financial goals. They can provide advice on budgeting, financing options, tax implications, and investment structuring. An advisor with expertise in real estate investments can offer valuable guidance on maximizing returns and minimizing risks.

Accountant: Navigating Taxes and Finances

An experienced accountant is crucial for handling the financial intricacies of property investment. They assist in managing property-related taxes, optimizing tax benefits, and ensuring compliance with financial regulations. Their expertise is especially important in structuring your investment in a tax-efficient manner.

Property Manager: Ensuring Efficient Management

If you're investing in rental property, a property manager can be a vital addition to your team. They handle day-to-day management tasks, including tenant screening, rent collection, maintenance, and addressing tenant issues. A competent property manager ensures your property is well-maintained and profitable.

Architect and Interior Designer: Maximizing Property Potential

For investments involving construction, renovation, or refurbishment, an architect and an interior designer are key. They help in maximizing the potential of your property, ensuring that any modifications or constructions are both aesthetically pleasing and functional, adding value to your investment.

Surveyor: Evaluating Property Condition

A surveyor assesses the condition of a property, identifying any structural issues or necessary repairs. Their evaluation is crucial, especially for older properties, and can influence your decision-making process and negotiation strategies.

Mortgage Broker: Financing Your Investment

If your investment strategy involves taking out a mortgage, a mortgage broker can be a useful asset. They help in finding the best financing options, negotiating terms, and guiding you through the mortgage application process.

Building a Cohesive Team

Building a reliable property investment team means choosing professionals who not only have the requisite expertise but also understand your investment goals and strategies. The key is to find individuals who communicate effectively, have a good reputation, and demonstrate a deep understanding of the Maltese real estate market.

The Role of Trust and Communication

Trust and open communication are fundamental in your relationship with your investment team. Regular meetings and updates can ensure everyone is on the same page, and your investment strategy is being followed effectively.

Continual Learning and Adaptation

The real estate market is dynamic, and your team should be capable of adapting to changing market conditions and regulations. Professionals who are committed to continual learning and staying abreast of market trends can provide you with cutting-edge advice and solutions.

Personal Involvement

While it's important to have experts on your team, your personal involvement is equally crucial. Stay informed and make decisions based on a combination of professional advice and your own research and instincts.

Evaluating Team Performance

Regularly assess the performance of your team members. This evaluation ensures that they continue to meet your needs and contribute positively to your investment goals. Don't hesitate to make changes in your team if necessary to align with your evolving investment strategy.

Collaboration for Success

Effective collaboration among your team members can significantly enhance the success of your investment. Encourage open dialogue and teamwork to leverage the diverse skills and perspectives each member brings to the table.

In building a reliable property investment team, the goal is to assemble a group of professionals who can provide comprehensive support and expert guidance. Each member plays a crucial role in different aspects of the investment process, contributing to the overall success of your real estate ventures in Malta. With a strong and cohesive team, you are well-equipped to navigate the complexities of the property market and achieve your investment objectives.

2.4: THE ROLE OF REAL ESTATE AGENTS IN MALTA

In the intricate world of property investment, real estate agents in Malta play a pivotal role. They serve as the conduit between buyers, sellers, and the Maltese real estate market. This section delves into the multifaceted role of real estate agents, highlighting how they can significantly influence your property investment experience.

Market Knowledge and Access

Real estate agents in Malta possess extensive knowledge of the local market. They are well-versed in current trends, property values, and the unique aspects of different Maltese localities. Agents have access to a wide array of listings, some of which may not be publicly available, offering you a broader selection of potential investments.

Professional Guidance and Advice

Agents provide professional guidance through every step of the property buying process. They can advise on the feasibility of investment opportunities, potential returns, and the pros and cons of different areas and property types. This advice is invaluable, especially for first-time investors or those unfamiliar with the Maltese market.

Negotiation and Mediation Skills

One of the key skills of real estate agents is their ability to negotiate and mediate. They represent your interests in negotiations, ensuring you get the best possible deal. Their experience in handling transactions can be critical in navigating complex negotiations and reaching a mutually beneficial agreement.

Facilitating Legal and Financial Processes

Although not legal experts, real estate agents help facilitate the legal and financial aspects of property transactions. They can guide you through the process of securing financing, understanding tax implications, and meeting legal requirements, such as the Acquisition of Immovable Property (AIP) permit for foreign buyers.

Handling Paperwork and Administrative Tasks

The purchase of property involves a significant amount of paperwork and administrative tasks. Agents assist in managing these tasks, ensuring that all documents are correctly completed and submitted on time. This assistance can be particularly helpful in avoiding common pitfalls and delays.

Building Networks and Contacts

Agents have extensive networks and contacts within the real estate industry. They can connect you with other professionals, such as lawyers, notaries, and architects, who are essential in the property buying process. This network can streamline your investment journey and provide additional support where needed.

Personalized Service and Understanding Client Needs

A good real estate agent offers personalized service, understanding and aligning with your specific needs and investment goals. They spend time getting to know your preferences, which enables them to present properties that closely match your criteria.

Market Exposure for Sellers

For those selling property, real estate agents provide valuable market exposure. They can effectively market your property, using their networks, marketing skills, and resources to reach potential buyers, both locally and internationally.

Keeping Up with Regulations and Trends

Real estate agents stay abreast of changes in regulations, laws, and market trends. This knowledge is crucial in providing clients with current and relevant advice, ensuring that investment decisions are made with the most up-to-date information.

Support Through the Buying Process

From viewing properties to closing the deal, agents support you throughout the buying process. They can schedule viewings, provide insights during property visits, and assist in understanding and completing purchase agreements.

After-Sale Services

The role of a real estate agent often extends beyond the purchase. They can offer after-sale services, such as advice on property management, rentals, and even resale opportunities, ensuring a continued relationship and support post-purchase.

Choosing the Right Agent

Selecting the right real estate agent is crucial. Look for agents with a solid reputation, a track record of successful transactions, and who are willing to go the extra mile to meet your needs. Personal recommendations, reviews, and interviews can help in making this choice.

Ethics and Professionalism

Professionalism and ethics are essential qualities in a real estate agent. Choose agents who are known for their integrity, honesty, and ethical conduct. This assurance is vital in building trust and ensuring a smooth investment process.

Communication and Responsiveness

Effective communication and responsiveness are key attributes of a good agent. They should be readily available to answer your queries, provide updates, and guide you through any challenges that arise during the investment process.

Adapting to Client's Changing Needs

An adept real estate agent is flexible and adaptable, able to adjust their approach based on the changing needs and circumstances of their clients. This adaptability is especially important in the dynamic real estate market of Malta.

In the Maltese real estate market, the role of real estate agents is integral to the success of property transactions. They offer a wealth of knowledge, skills, and resources, making them indispensable allies in your property investment journey. By understanding their role and selecting the right agent, you can navigate the complexities of the Maltese property market with confidence and efficiency.

2.5: UNDERSTANDING THE MALTESE PROPERTY INVESTMENT LANGUAGE

Venturing into the Maltese real estate market requires more than just an understanding of property types and market trends; it necessitates a grasp of the specific language and terms used in the local property investment sector. This section is dedicated to demystifying the language of Maltese property investment, providing clarity on key terms, legal jargon, and local phrases that are pivotal in making informed decisions.

Key Terms in Property Transactions

The Maltese property market, like any other, has its set of unique terms. Familiarizing yourself with these terms is crucial for effective communication with agents, lawyers, and other real estate professionals. Terms such as 'Freehold' and 'Leasehold' are fundamental in understanding property ownership rights. 'Freehold' indicates full ownership of the property and the land it stands on, while 'Leasehold' involves owning the property for a fixed term, with the land remaining under someone else's ownership.

Understanding 'Konvenju'

A critical term in Maltese property transactions is 'Konvenju,' or the Promise of Sale Agreement. This legal agreement outlines the terms and conditions agreed upon by the buyer and seller, and it sets the stage for the final deed of sale. Understanding the components of a 'Konvenju,' including deposit requirements, stipulated conditions, and timeframes, is essential for any property transaction in Malta.

Legal Jargon in Property Investment

Legal jargon can often be perplexing, especially in a foreign real estate market. Terms such as 'Notary Public,' 'AIP Permit' (Acquisition of Immovable Property Permit), and 'Hypothec' (a legal charge on property) are commonly used in Maltese property transactions. Grasping these terms ensures that you understand the legal processes and requirements of buying or selling property in Malta.

Property Descriptions and Features

Understanding property descriptions is vital when exploring investment options. Terms describing property features such as 'terraced house,' 'maisonette,' or 'penthouse' provide insight into the layout and style of the property. Local architectural features like 'Gallarija' (enclosed wooden balcony) and 'Mdina glass' add to the charm and value of Maltese properties.

Financial Terms and Taxation

Navigating the financial aspect of property investment involves understanding terms related to taxation and financing. Familiarity with terms such as 'Stamp Duty,' 'Capital Gains Tax,' and 'Loan-to-Value Ratio' (LTV) is imperative. Knowing these terms helps in comprehending the financial implications of your property investment, including potential taxes and mortgage options.

Rental Market Terminology

For those investing in rental properties, understanding terms specific to the rental market is essential. Phrases like 'gross rental yield,' 'tenancy agreement,' and 'landlord obligations' are part of the everyday vocabulary in property leasing and management.

Terms Related to Property Development and Construction

If your investment involves property development or renovation, terms related to construction and development become relevant. Understanding terms like 'planning permission,' 'building regulations,' and 'environmental impact assessment' is crucial for any development project in Malta.

Local Phrases and Cultural Nuances

The Maltese language and culture also influence the property market. Local phrases and colloquial terms often surface in property listings and discussions. While not all may be directly related to the technical aspects of property investment, understanding these nuances can enhance your interaction with locals and enrich your investment experience.

Regular Updates and Continued Learning

The language of property investment is not static; new terms and concepts emerge as the market evolves. Staying updated with the latest terminology and market trends is important for keeping pace with the dynamic nature of real estate in Malta.

Utilizing Resources for Learning

Various resources are available to aid in learning the language of Maltese property investment. Real estate websites, legal guides, and investment seminars are valuable sources of information. Engaging with these resources can significantly improve your understanding and comfort level with the local property investment language.

Professional Assistance

While self-education is beneficial, seeking assistance from professionals when faced with unfamiliar terms or complex jargon is advisable. Real estate agents, lawyers, and financial advisors can provide explanations and guidance, ensuring that language barriers do not hinder your investment decisions.

Effective Communication

Effective communication is key in property investment. Understanding and using the correct terminology can facilitate smoother transactions and interactions with all parties involved in your investment journey.

Cultural Sensitivity and Respect

Embracing the local language and culture with sensitivity and respect can greatly enhance your property investment experience in Malta. It demonstrates your commitment and willingness to integrate into the local market, fostering positive relationships with professionals and locals alike.

Understanding the Maltese property investment language is an integral part of successful real estate ventures in Malta. This knowledge not only aids in navigating the market but also enhances your ability to make informed decisions, communicate effectively, and engage with the local real estate community. By familiarizing yourself with the specific terms and jargon used in the Maltese property market, you are better equipped to embark on a rewarding investment journey.

CHAPTER 3:
FINANCIAL CONSIDERATIONS IN PROPERTY INVESTMENT

Delving into property investment is not just about selecting the right property; it's fundamentally about understanding and managing the financial implications that come with it. In this chapter, we'll explore the critical financial aspects of property investment in Malta. From comprehending the various taxes and fees associated with Maltese real estate to navigating through financing options, the impact of interest rates, and budgeting for unforeseen costs, this chapter aims to equip you with a thorough understanding of the financial landscape. We will also delve into strategies for maximizing your investment returns, ensuring that your journey in property investment is both financially sound and rewarding.

3.1: UNDERSTANDING TAXES AND FEES IN MALTA'S REAL ESTATE

Navigating through the landscape of taxes and fees is a crucial aspect of property investment in Malta. A clear understanding of these financial obligations not only helps in budgeting accurately but also ensures compliance with local regulations. This section aims to demystify the various taxes and fees associated with buying, owning, and selling property in Malta.

Stamp Duty

One of the primary costs when purchasing property in Malta is the stamp duty. This is a tax paid by the buyer on the acquisition of property. The standard rate is typically 5% of the property's purchase price, but there are certain conditions and exceptions where this rate may vary. For instance, first-time buyers may benefit from reduced rates or exemptions under specific programs.

Notarial Fees

Notarial fees are another significant expense in property transactions. A notary in Malta is responsible for drafting the contract, conducting searches to ensure clear title, and registering the property. The fees for these services are usually a percentage of the property price and can vary depending on the complexity of the transaction.

Legal Fees

Legal fees are incurred when engaging a lawyer to oversee the transaction. While not mandatory, having legal representation is advisable, particularly for more complex transactions or for foreign investors unfamiliar with Maltese property law. Legal fees are typically based on the property's purchase price and the scope of services provided.

Real Estate Agency Fees

If a real estate agent is involved in the transaction, their fees, usually borne by the seller, are another cost to consider. These fees are typically a percentage of the sale price and are only payable upon the successful completion of the sale.

Capital Gains Tax

When selling a property in Malta, Capital Gains Tax (CGT) may apply. This tax is levied on the profit made from the sale, calculated as the difference between the selling price and the original purchase price, after adjusting for inflation and certain deductible expenses. The specific rate and exemptions can vary, making it essential to understand the current tax laws.

Property Transfer Tax

Alternatively, sellers might opt to pay a Property Transfer Tax instead of CGT, which is calculated as a percentage of the selling price. The decision between CGT and Property Transfer Tax depends on various factors, including how long the property was held and the amount of profit made.

Value Added Tax (VAT)

In Malta, VAT is generally not applicable to residential property transactions. However, it is applicable to the purchase of new buildings from a developer and on certain professional fees. Understanding the VAT implications is important, especially for investors dealing with commercial properties or new developments.

Local Council Taxes and Utility Bills

Owning a property in Malta also involves ongoing costs like local council taxes and utility bills. Council taxes are relatively low and contribute to local services and amenities. Utility bills in Malta, covering electricity, water, and waste services, are additional recurring expenses that property owners need to budget for.

Annual Property Taxes

Unlike many other countries, Malta does not impose annual property taxes on residential properties. This is a significant benefit for property owners and investors, reducing the ongoing cost of owning property in Malta.

Insurance Costs

Property insurance, while not legally mandatory, is highly recommended. Insurance policies cover various risks, including damage from natural disasters, theft, and liability. The cost of insurance varies based on the property value, location, and coverage extent.

Special Contributions for Common Areas

In properties like apartments and condominiums, there may be fees for the upkeep of common areas, known as condominium or common area fees. These fees cover maintenance and repairs of shared spaces such as elevators, gardens, and swimming pools.

Maintenance and Renovation Costs

Ongoing maintenance and potential renovation costs are important financial considerations. Regular maintenance keeps the property in good condition and can prevent costly repairs in the future. Renovation or upgrades can also be significant, especially for older properties or those purchased as investment projects.

Understanding the Full Financial Picture

Investing in Maltese real estate requires a comprehensive understanding of all associated taxes and fees. Being aware of these costs upfront helps in making more accurate budgeting and investment decisions. It's advisable to consult with financial experts and real estate professionals to get a clear understanding of all the costs involved in your specific property transaction.

Staying Updated with Tax Laws and Regulations

Tax laws and regulations can change, and staying updated with these changes is crucial for property investors. Keeping abreast of current laws ensures that you remain compliant and can make the most of any tax benefits or exemptions available.

A thorough grasp of the various taxes and fees associated with property investment in Malta is fundamental. It not only aids in effective financial planning but also ensures a smoother transaction process. By accounting for these expenses, investors can develop a more accurate picture of their potential investment returns and make informed decisions in the Maltese property market.

3.2: FINANCING OPTIONS FOR PROPERTY INVESTMENT

Exploring the realm of property investment in Malta necessitates a clear understanding of the various financing options available. Securing the right type of financing is crucial as it impacts the overall profitability and feasibility of the investment. This section aims to provide a comprehensive overview of the financing avenues you can consider for property investment in Malta.

Mortgages and Loans

The most common way to finance property investments in Malta is through mortgages. Banks and financial institutions offer various mortgage products, each with different interest rates, terms, and conditions. When considering a mortgage, it's important to understand the different types – fixed-rate, variable-rate, and interest-only mortgages, and how they align with your investment strategy.

Loan-to-Value Ratio (LTV)

The Loan-to-Value Ratio is a critical factor in mortgage financing. It represents the percentage of the property's value that the bank is willing to finance. In Malta, banks typically offer an LTV of up to 70-80% for residential properties. Higher LTV ratios may be available, but they often come with higher interest rates or additional requirements.

Interest Rates and Repayment Terms

Interest rates and repayment terms vary significantly between financial institutions. Some offer lower rates but with shorter repayment terms, while others may provide longer terms but at higher rates. It's essential to compare different mortgage products to find the one that best suits your financial situation and investment goals.

Government-Backed Loans and Schemes

The Maltese government occasionally offers loan schemes and incentives to encourage property investment, particularly for first-time buyers or specific demographics. These schemes may offer favorable terms, such as lower interest rates or reduced down payment requirements, making property investment more accessible.

Private Lenders and Financing

Apart from banks, private lenders are another source of financing. These lenders might provide more flexible terms and quicker processing times but often at higher interest rates. Private financing can be a viable option for investors who may not qualify for traditional bank loans or need funds more rapidly.

Equity Release

For those who already own property, equity release is an option where you can borrow against the value of your existing property. This can be a way to finance a new property investment without selling your current assets. However, it's important to carefully consider the risks and implications of using your home as collateral.

Joint Ventures and Partnerships

Entering into a joint venture or partnership can be a strategic way to finance a property investment. This approach involves pooling resources with other investors, which can increase your buying power and share the risks. It's crucial to have clear agreements and understandings with partners to avoid conflicts.

Crowdfunding Platforms

Real estate crowdfunding has emerged as an innovative financing option. Through crowdfunding platforms, investors can pool funds with others to invest in property. While this reduces individual risk and financial commitment, it's important to understand the platform's terms, fees, and the nature of the investment.

Self-Financing and Personal Savings

For some investors, using personal savings or self-financing can be the most straightforward option. This approach eliminates interest payments and loan obligations, but it also involves tying up a significant amount of personal capital in the investment.

Foreign Financing

Foreign nationals looking to invest in Malta might consider financing options available in their home country. This could include taking out a loan in their home country and using it to finance a property in Malta. However, this option requires understanding the implications of foreign exchange rates and international financial regulations.

Assessing Your Financial Position

Before deciding on a financing option, it's crucial to assess your financial position. Consider your current assets, liabilities, cash flow, and how the investment aligns with your long-term financial goals. A solid financial plan ensures that your property investment does not overextend your financial capabilities.

Professional Financial Advice

Given the complexities and variety of financing options, consulting with a financial advisor is advisable. A professional can help you navigate through the options, assess their suitability for your investment plan, and guide you in making an informed decision.

Preparing for Loan Application

When applying for a loan or mortgage, being well-prepared is key. This includes having all necessary documentation, such as proof of income, assets, and a good credit history. A strong application increases your chances of securing favorable financing terms.

Considering the Overall Cost of Financing

In addition to the principal amount, consider the overall cost of financing, including interest, fees, and any other charges. This comprehensive understanding helps in evaluating the true cost of the loan and its impact on your investment returns.

Selecting the right financing option for property investment in Malta requires a careful evaluation of various factors, including interest rates, terms, and your financial health. By thoroughly exploring and understanding the available financing avenues, you can make a choice that not only supports your property acquisition but also aligns with your broader investment strategy and financial goals.

3.3: THE IMPACT OF INTEREST RATES ON PROPERTY INVESTMENTS

Interest rates play a critical role in the realm of property investment, influencing both the cost of borrowing and the overall return on investment. Understanding the impact of interest rates is essential for any investor in the Maltese real estate market. This section explores how interest rates affect property investments and strategies to mitigate their impact.

Interest Rates and Mortgage Payments

For most property investors, the most direct impact of interest rates is on mortgage payments. Higher interest rates mean higher monthly payments on variable-rate mortgages, directly affecting cash flow and the affordability of an investment. For those with fixed-rate mortgages, the impact is felt when refinancing or purchasing new properties.

Effect on Property Values

Interest rates can also affect property values. Generally, higher interest rates lead to increased borrowing costs, which can reduce the demand for property and, consequently, lower property values. Conversely, lower interest rates can stimulate property markets, as borrowing is more affordable, potentially increasing demand and property values.

Rental Yields vs. Interest Rates

For investments in rental properties, the relationship between rental yields and interest rates is key. When interest rates rise, rental yields must also increase to remain attractive to investors. If rental income does not keep pace with rising interest rates, the investment may become less profitable.

Investor Sentiment and Market Dynamics

Interest rates can influence investor sentiment and overall market dynamics. Lower interest rates often encourage more investment in real estate, as alternative investment options like savings accounts or bonds offer lower returns. Conversely, when interest rates rise, real estate investments might be seen as less attractive compared to other investment avenues.

Leverage and Interest Rate Risk

Leverage, or the use of borrowed capital for investment, amplifies the impact of interest rates. High leverage can lead to greater returns in a low-interest-rate environment but can also increase risk significantly if rates rise. Understanding this relationship is crucial in managing the risk associated with leveraged property investments.

Variable vs. Fixed-Rate Mortgages

Choosing between a variable and a fixed-rate mortgage is a significant decision influenced by interest rate expectations. Fixed-rate mortgages offer certainty over repayments but can be more expensive in the short term. Variable rates offer lower initial rates but with the risk of increase over time.

Impact on Refinancing Decisions

For those looking to refinance existing property investments, interest rates are a critical factor. Lower rates can make refinancing attractive, offering opportunities to reduce repayments or release equity. However, rising rates can increase the cost of refinancing and reduce its appeal.

Inflation and Real Interest Rates

Understanding the relationship between inflation and nominal interest rates is important. Real interest rates (nominal interest rates adjusted for inflation) provide a clearer picture of the cost of borrowing and the real return on investment. Inflation can erode the value of future rental income and property values, impacting investment returns.

Interest Rates and Investment Strategies

Different investment strategies have varying sensitivities to interest rate changes. For example, strategies focused on capital appreciation may be more vulnerable to interest rate increases than those focused on generating steady rental income.

Central Bank Policies and Economic Factors

Interest rates are influenced by central bank policies and economic factors. Keeping abreast of economic trends and monetary policy decisions can provide insights into future interest rate movements, aiding in strategic planning and decision-making.

Diversification as a Risk Management Tool

Diversification can be an effective strategy to manage interest rate risk. By investing in a mix of properties with different financing structures or in different geographical areas with varying interest rate exposures, investors can mitigate the impact of rate changes.

Fixed-Rate Lock-Ins and Hedging Strategies

For those concerned about rising rates, locking in a fixed interest rate or using financial instruments to hedge against interest rate fluctuations can be viable strategies. These options provide predictability and protect against adverse interest rate movements.

Interest Rate Forecasts and Market Timing

While forecasting interest rate movements is challenging, keeping informed about economic forecasts and market trends can provide valuable insights. Timing investment decisions to capitalize on favorable interest rate environments can enhance investment returns.

Assessing Affordability in Different Rate Scenarios

It's prudent for investors to assess the affordability of their investments under different interest rate scenarios. This involves calculating the potential impact of rate changes on mortgage repayments and cash flow.

Long-Term Perspective and Interest Rates

Adopting a long-term perspective can help mitigate the short-term impact of interest rate fluctuations. Property investment is typically a long-term endeavor, and short-term rate changes may have less impact over the longer term.

Understanding the impact of interest rates on property investments is crucial for making informed decisions in the real estate market. By considering the various ways in which interest rates can affect investment returns, property values, and financing costs, investors can develop strategies to navigate this complex aspect of property investment. Staying informed and adaptable to interest rate changes ensures a more resilient and successful investment approach.

3.4: BUDGETING FOR ADDITIONAL COSTS

Effective budgeting for additional costs is a critical aspect of successful property investment. Beyond the purchase price, numerous other expenses can affect the overall profitability and viability of your investment. This section provides an in-depth exploration of the various additional costs associated with property investment in Malta, emphasizing the importance of comprehensive budget planning.

Renovation and Repair Costs

One of the most significant additional costs in property investment is for renovations and repairs. Whether it's updating an older property, making repairs, or customizing a new investment to suit your needs, these costs can be substantial. Allocating a realistic budget for renovations is crucial, taking into consideration the property's age, condition, and your long-term investment goals.

Furniture and Fittings

For investors planning to rent out their property, or those purchasing a holiday home, budgeting for furniture and fittings is essential. The cost can vary widely depending on the quality and extent of furnishings required. It's important to strike a balance between durability, aesthetics, and cost-effectiveness.

Property Management Fees

If you intend to hire a property manager, especially for rental properties, factor in property management fees. These fees cover the cost of managing tenants, maintenance, rent collection, and other day-to-day management tasks. Typically, these fees are a percentage of the rental income.

Insurance Costs

Property insurance is a vital but often overlooked expense. Insurance protects against risks like fire, natural disasters, and liability claims. The cost depends on the property's value, location, and the type of coverage you choose. Adequate insurance is essential to protect your investment.

Utility Connections and Ongoing Bills

Setting up and maintaining utility services is another cost consideration. This includes connection fees for services like electricity, water, and internet, as well as ongoing monthly bills. For rental properties, decide whether these costs will be included in the rent or charged separately to tenants.

Council Taxes and Community Fees

Council taxes and community fees contribute to local services and amenities maintenance. While these fees are generally not prohibitive in Malta, they should be included in your budget. For properties in developments or condominiums, there may be additional fees for the upkeep of shared spaces and facilities.

Legal and Administrative Fees

Legal and administrative fees can accumulate during the purchase process and beyond. This includes fees for legal counsel, notary services, and any administrative costs associated with property registration and compliance with local regulations.

Marketing and Advertising Expenses

For rental properties, budgeting for marketing and advertising is crucial to attract tenants. This might include costs for listing the property online, professional photography, or engaging a rental agent.

Contingency Fund

A contingency fund is essential for unexpected expenses or to cover periods when the property may be vacant. A general rule of thumb is to set aside a percentage of the property value or rental income to cover such contingencies.

Long-term Maintenance and Upkeep

Budgeting for long-term maintenance and upkeep is critical to preserve the property's value and appeal. This includes regular cleaning, painting, appliance replacements, and structural repairs. A well-maintained property is more attractive to tenants and can command higher rental rates.

Interest and Financing Costs

If you are financing your investment through a mortgage or loan, the interest and associated financing costs should be factored into your budget. These costs can vary depending on the loan terms and interest rate fluctuations.

Potential Vacancy Periods

For rental properties, it's prudent to budget for potential vacancy periods. This means having enough reserves to cover mortgage payments, utilities, and other expenses during times when the property is not generating rental income.

Tax Implications and Obligations

Understanding and budgeting for tax implications, including income tax on rental earnings and capital gains tax on property sales, is important. Consulting with a tax professional can help you understand these obligations and plan accordingly.

Inflation and Cost Increases

Consider the impact of inflation and potential cost increases over time. Expenses like utility bills, property taxes, and maintenance costs may rise, and your budget should account for these potential increases.

Reviewing and Adjusting Your Budget

Regularly reviewing and adjusting your budget is important as costs can change over time. Staying informed about market trends, maintenance requirements, and operational costs helps in keeping your budget up-to-date.

Professional Advice

Seeking advice from financial advisors or property experts can provide valuable insights into budgeting effectively for your property investment. Professional advice can help you anticipate and plan for costs you might not have considered.

Budgeting for additional costs is a crucial element of property investment, requiring careful planning and consideration. By accounting for these expenses, you can create a more accurate and realistic financial plan, ensuring your investment remains profitable and sustainable over the long term. Effective budget management not only protects your investment but also enhances its potential for success.

3.5: INVESTMENT STRATEGIES FOR MAXIMUM RETURNS

Maximizing returns on property investment requires strategic planning and an understanding of the various factors that influence real estate profitability. This section explores different investment strategies in the Maltese property market, offering insights into how investors can optimize their returns while mitigating risks.

Choosing the Right Location

Location is a pivotal factor in property investment. In Malta, certain areas offer higher potential for capital appreciation due to factors like development projects, tourist appeal, or business growth. Investing in emerging neighborhoods or areas slated for future development can yield significant returns as property values increase over time.

Buy-and-Hold Strategy

A popular investment strategy is the buy-and-hold approach, where investors purchase property and hold onto it for an extended period. This strategy benefits from long-term capital growth and can provide steady rental income. The key is to select properties in areas with strong potential for appreciation and stable rental demand.

Value-Added Investments

Value-added investment involves purchasing properties that require upgrades or renovations. By improving the property, investors can increase its value and rental appeal. This strategy requires an understanding of renovation costs and the types of improvements that add the most value.

Short-Term Rentals and Vacation Properties

With Malta's thriving tourism industry, investing in short-term rentals or vacation properties can be lucrative. These properties often command higher rental rates than long-term rentals, though they may require more active management and marketing efforts.

Diversification of Property Types

Diversifying your investment portfolio across different types of properties, such as residential, commercial, or mixed-use, can spread risk and increase potential returns. Each property type has its own market dynamics and risk factors, and a diversified portfolio can balance these elements.

Leveraging Market Cycles

Understanding and leveraging real estate market cycles can significantly impact investment returns. Buying properties during a market downturn and selling during a market upswing can maximize capital gains. Staying informed about market trends and economic indicators is crucial for timing these cycles effectively.

Utilizing Tax Benefits and Incentives

Taking advantage of tax benefits and government incentives can increase investment returns. In Malta, various programs and schemes offer tax incentives, reduced stamp duties, or other benefits for property investors. Understanding these opportunities and incorporating them into your investment strategy is important.

Focus on Cash Flow Management

Effective cash flow management is vital for maximizing returns. This involves not only ensuring a steady stream of rental income but also managing expenses like maintenance, taxes, and mortgage payments. Positive cash flow ensures that the investment remains sustainable and profitable.

Strategic Refinancing

Refinancing can be a strategic tool for maximizing returns. By refinancing to a lower interest rate or tapping into property equity, investors can reduce costs or free up capital for additional investments. This strategy requires a careful assessment of refinancing costs and market conditions.

Active Property Management

Active property management, whether self-managed or through a professional manager, can enhance investment returns. Efficient management includes regular maintenance, tenant relations, and effective marketing to minimize vacancies and maximize rental income.

Long-Term Perspective

Adopting a long-term perspective in property investment can lead to greater returns. Real estate is typically a long-haul investment, and a patient approach can yield significant benefits as property values grow over time.

Continuous Market Research

Ongoing market research is essential for staying ahead of trends, understanding shifts in demand, and identifying new investment opportunities. Staying informed about developments in the Maltese property market, economic factors, and changes in legislation can provide a competitive edge.

Risk Management

Effective risk management is key to maximizing returns. This involves diversifying investments, understanding market risks, and preparing for potential downturns. A risk-averse strategy ensures that your investments can withstand market fluctuations.

Building Networks and Relationships

Building strong networks and relationships in the real estate industry can provide access to valuable information, off-market deals, and partnership opportunities. Networking with agents, investors, and industry professionals can open doors to unique investment opportunities.

Professional Guidance

Seeking professional guidance from real estate experts, financial advisors, and tax professionals can enhance your investment strategy. Professional advice can provide insights into market dynamics, legal considerations, and financial planning, contributing to informed decision-making.

Implementing strategic investment approaches tailored to the Maltese property market can significantly enhance the potential for maximum returns. By carefully considering location, market trends, property types, financial management, and risk factors, investors can develop robust strategies that capitalize on the opportunities in Malta's dynamic real estate landscape. An informed and well-planned approach to property investment is essential for achieving long-term success and optimal returns.

CHAPTER 4:
LEGAL FRAMEWORK AND COMPLIANCE

Navigating the legal framework and ensuring compliance is a fundamental aspect of successful property investment in Malta. This chapter aims to provide a comprehensive guide to the legal intricacies of Maltese real estate. From understanding property laws and regulations to ensuring adherence to legal requirements throughout the investment process, we delve into the critical aspects that govern property transactions in Malta. Emphasizing the importance of legal due diligence, this chapter serves as a roadmap for investors to securely and confidently engage with the Maltese property market, ensuring their investments are protected and compliant with all legal standards.

4.1: NAVIGATING MALTA'S PROPERTY LAWS

Understanding and navigating Malta's property laws is crucial for anyone involved in the real estate market. These laws govern the various aspects of property ownership, sale, purchase, and development in Malta. This section outlines the key legal frameworks and regulations that investors and property owners need to be aware of.

The Legal Framework of Property Ownership

Malta's legal system, influenced by both Roman law and British law, provides a robust framework for property ownership and transactions. The primary legislation governing property transactions is the Civil Code, which outlines the rights and obligations of property owners.

Contract of Sale

In Malta, a property sale is legally binding when both parties sign a contract of sale (konvenju). This agreement outlines the terms of the sale, including the price, property description, and any conditions. It is a legally binding document and is essential in the transfer of property ownership.

Promise of Sale Agreement (Konvenju)

Before the final contract, a preliminary agreement, or konvenju, is typically signed. This agreement sets out the terms and conditions of the sale and binds both the buyer and the seller for a specified period, usually three months. During this time, due diligence is carried out.

Due Diligence in Property Transactions

Due diligence is a critical part of property transactions in Malta. This includes title searches to verify the owner's right to sell, checking for any encumbrances or liens on the property, and ensuring compliance with planning and building regulations.

Acquisition of Immovable Property (AIP) Permit

Non-residents and non-Maltese citizens may require an Acquisition of Immovable Property (AIP) permit to buy property in Malta. This permit is necessary for specific areas and for certain types of properties. It ensures that the acquisition complies with Maltese law regarding foreign property ownership.

Property Registration

Property registration in Malta is conducted through the Public Registry and the Land Registry. These registries record property ownership, transactions, and any legal burdens on the property. Registration provides legal certainty and public transparency of property ownership.

Notarial Role in Property Transactions

Notaries in Malta play a crucial role in property transactions. They are responsible for drafting the property sale agreement, conducting due diligence, and ensuring that the transaction complies with all legal requirements. The notary also registers the deed of sale with the relevant authorities.

Taxes and Fees in Property Transactions

Understanding the tax implications and fees associated with property transactions is essential. This includes stamp duty, capital gains tax, and notarial fees. These costs can significantly affect the overall investment and should be factored into financial planning.

Rental Laws

For investors interested in rental properties, understanding Malta's rental laws is important. These laws govern the relationship between landlords and tenants, rental agreements, rent increases, and tenant rights.

Planning and Development Regulations

Compliance with planning and development regulations is essential for property development in Malta. The Planning Authority oversees these regulations, ensuring that developments adhere to zoning laws, building standards, and environmental considerations.

Heritage and Conservation Regulations

Malta has strict regulations regarding the preservation of its rich historical and cultural heritage. Properties in designated conservation areas or historical buildings are subject to additional regulations and restrictions.

Legal Representation

Given the complexity of Maltese property laws, engaging a lawyer with expertise in real estate law is advisable. Legal representation ensures that all aspects of the transaction are compliant with Maltese law and that your legal rights are protected.

Understanding Lease Agreements

For leased properties, understanding the legalities of lease agreements is important. This includes the terms of the lease, rights and obligations of both landlord and tenant, and conditions for lease termination.

Dispute Resolution

In the event of a dispute, Malta's legal system provides mechanisms for resolution, including litigation and arbitration. Understanding the dispute resolution process is important for property owners and investors.

Staying Informed About Legal Changes

Property laws in Malta can evolve, with new legislation and amendments being introduced. Staying informed about legal changes is important for anyone involved in the property market.

Environmental and Building Regulations

Compliance with environmental and building regulations is also a key legal consideration. These regulations ensure that property developments are sustainable, safe, and environmentally responsible.

Navigating Malta's property laws requires a comprehensive understanding of the legal landscape. From the initial agreement to post-purchase compliance, each step involves specific legal considerations. Being well-informed and seeking professional legal advice is vital for successful property transactions in Malta, ensuring that investments are secure and legally compliant.

4.2: THE ROLE OF LEGAL COUNSEL IN PROPERTY TRANSACTIONS

In the intricate world of property investment, the role of legal counsel is indispensable. Engaging a lawyer specialized in real estate law can significantly streamline the process, ensuring that all legal aspects of the transaction are handled efficiently and correctly. This section delves into the multifaceted role of legal counsel in property transactions in Malta, highlighting their importance in both safeguarding your investment and ensuring compliance with local laws and regulations.

Ensuring Legal Compliance

One of the primary roles of legal counsel in property transactions is to ensure that all aspects of the deal comply with Maltese law. This includes verifying property titles, ensuring that the terms of the sale are legally binding, and checking for any outstanding legal issues that could affect the transaction.

Drafting and Reviewing Contracts

Legal counsel is responsible for drafting and reviewing contracts related to the property transaction. This includes the initial Promise of Sale agreement (Konvenju) and the final deed of sale. They ensure that the contracts accurately reflect the terms agreed upon and protect the client's interests.

Conducting Due Diligence

A thorough due diligence process is crucial in property transactions. Legal counsel conducts extensive research to verify the property's legal status, including checking for any encumbrances, liens, or outstanding debts associated with the property. They also ensure that the property complies with local planning and zoning regulations.

Negotiating Terms and Conditions

Lawyers play a vital role in negotiating the terms and conditions of the property transaction. They work to secure the most favorable terms for their clients, addressing issues such as price, payment schedules, and any contingent clauses that need to be included in the contract.

Handling Property Registration

After the completion of the sale, legal counsel handles the registration of the property. This involves submitting the necessary documents to the Public Registry and ensuring that the transfer of ownership is officially recorded.

Advising on Tax Implications

Understanding the tax implications of a property transaction is crucial. Legal counsel provides advice on matters such as stamp duty, capital gains tax, and any potential tax benefits or exemptions that may be applicable to the client.

Assisting with Financing and Mortgages

For transactions involving mortgages or other types of financing, legal counsel assists in navigating the terms and conditions of the loan. They ensure that the mortgage documents are in order and that their clients understand their financial obligations.

Dealing with Specialized Transactions

In cases involving specialized transactions, such as buying property through a company, inheritance issues, or purchasing property as a foreign national, legal counsel provides expert advice and guidance tailored to these specific scenarios.

Resolving Disputes

If disputes arise during the property transaction, legal counsel represents their clients' interests. They employ negotiation, mediation, or litigation strategies to resolve issues effectively.

Providing Ongoing Legal Support

The role of legal counsel often extends beyond the completion of the property transaction. They provide ongoing legal support, advising on matters such as property management, lease agreements, and any future legal issues that may arise.

Ensuring Ethical Conduct

Legal counsel ensures that all parties involved in the transaction adhere to ethical standards and legal practices. They maintain confidentiality and act in the best interest of their clients throughout the transaction process.

Advising on Property Development Projects

For clients involved in property development, legal counsel advises on a range of issues including land acquisition, construction contracts, regulatory compliance, and environmental considerations.

Facilitating International Transactions

For foreign investors, legal counsel plays a critical role in facilitating international property transactions. They help navigate the complexities of cross-border investments, ensuring compliance with both local and international laws.

Risk Assessment and Management

A key aspect of legal counsel's role is to assess and manage risks associated with property transactions. They identify potential legal risks and advise on strategies to mitigate them, protecting their client's investment.

Adapting to Legal Changes

The legal landscape in real estate is dynamic, with laws and regulations frequently changing. Legal counsel stays abreast of these changes, ensuring that their clients' transactions remain compliant and their advice is current.

The role of legal counsel in property transactions is multifaceted and vital for the success of any real estate investment in Malta. They provide the expertise and guidance necessary to navigate the legal complexities of property transactions, ensuring that the process is conducted smoothly, efficiently, and in compliance with all relevant laws. By engaging competent legal counsel, investors and property buyers can safeguard their interests and ensure a secure and legally sound investment.

4.3: UNDERSTANDING CONTRACTS AND AGREEMENTS

In property transactions, contracts and agreements are the legal backbone, defining the rights and obligations of all parties involved. A deep understanding of these documents is crucial for anyone engaging in the Maltese property market. This section aims to shed light on the various types of contracts and agreements encountered in property transactions, emphasizing their significance and the need for careful scrutiny.

Promise of Sale Agreement (Konvenju)

The Konvenju is a preliminary agreement between the buyer and seller, marking the initial commitment to the transaction. It outlines the terms of the sale, including the price, property description, and any conditions to be met before the final deed. Understanding the Konvenju is critical as it legally binds both parties to the transaction.

Final Deed of Sale

The Final Deed of Sale is the conclusive legal document that transfers property ownership. It is executed once all conditions in the Konvenju are satisfied. The deed should reflect all the terms agreed upon in the Konvenju, and it's essential to review it carefully to ensure accuracy and completeness.

Due Diligence in Contract Review

Thorough due diligence in reviewing contracts is vital. This involves checking for any discrepancies between the Konvenju and the final deed, ensuring that all terms are clearly stated, and verifying that there are no hidden clauses or unexpected obligations.

Clauses and Conditions

Contracts often contain various clauses and conditions that can significantly impact the transaction. These may include penalty clauses for delayed completion, clauses regarding the property's condition, and provisions for backing out of the deal. Understanding these clauses is crucial to protect your interests.

Mortgage Agreements

If the property purchase involves a mortgage, the mortgage agreement is a key document. It outlines the terms of the loan, including the interest rate, repayment schedule, and any penalties for early repayment. Scrutinizing the mortgage agreement is necessary to understand your financial commitments fully.

Rental Agreements

For investment properties, rental agreements define the relationship between landlord and tenant. Key aspects include the rental amount, duration of the lease, tenant and landlord responsibilities, and conditions for termination. A well-drafted rental agreement is essential for avoiding future disputes.

Leasehold Agreements

In leasehold property transactions, understanding the leasehold agreement is crucial. This agreement sets out the terms under which the property is leased, including the duration of the lease, ground rent, and any restrictions on the use of the property.

Building and Renovation Contracts

For properties requiring construction or renovation, contracts with builders and contractors are important. These contracts should detail the scope of work, timelines, costs, and payment terms. They should also include provisions for handling delays, cost overruns, and quality disputes.

Insurance Contracts

Insurance contracts for property coverage are essential to protect against unforeseen damages. Understanding the extent of coverage, exclusions, and the claims process is vital to ensure adequate protection for your investment.

Joint Ownership Agreements

In cases of joint ownership, a joint ownership agreement can delineate the rights and responsibilities of each owner, including contributions to costs, division of income, and procedures for selling the property.

Understanding Legal Jargon

Contracts often contain legal jargon that can be difficult to interpret. Familiarity with legal terminology used in property contracts is crucial for understanding your rights and obligations.

Professional Legal Review

Given the complexity of property contracts, engaging a legal professional to review and explain the terms is advisable. A lawyer can identify potential issues, suggest amendments, and ensure that the contract aligns with your best interests.

Amendments and Negotiations

Contracts are not always set in stone and can often be amended through negotiations. If certain terms are not favorable, it's possible to renegotiate these aspects before signing the agreement.

Record Keeping

Maintaining a record of all contracts and agreements is important for future reference. This includes keeping copies of the signed documents and any correspondence related to the transaction.

Cultural and Language Considerations

For foreign investors, understanding contracts may also involve dealing with language barriers. Ensuring that contracts are available in a language you are fluent in is important to avoid misunderstandings.

Understanding contracts and agreements in property transactions is a fundamental aspect of investing in real estate. It involves careful review, comprehension of legal terms, and often the assistance of legal professionals. By thoroughly understanding these documents, you can ensure that your property transactions are conducted smoothly and that your interests are adequately protected.

4.4: PROPERTY RIGHTS AND OWNERSHIP REGULATIONS

Understanding property rights and ownership regulations is crucial in the realm of real estate investment, particularly in a distinct market like Malta. These regulations define the legalities of owning and using property, impacting everything from the purchase process to the rights of owners and tenants. This section delves into the key aspects of property rights and ownership regulations in Malta, highlighting their importance in ensuring secure and lawful property transactions.

Types of Property Ownership

In Malta, property ownership is primarily classified as either freehold or leasehold. Freehold ownership implies complete control over the property without time constraints, whereas leasehold refers to owning a property for a fixed period, after which the property reverts to the freeholder. Understanding the type of ownership is vital, as it affects your rights over the property.

Acquisition of Immovable Property (AIP) Permit

Foreign nationals looking to purchase property in Malta often require an AIP permit. This permit is necessary for specific regions and property types, intended to regulate foreign ownership of Maltese property. The AIP outlines conditions for foreign buyers, including minimum value thresholds and commitments to retain the property for a minimum period.

Succession and Inheritance Laws

Malta's succession and inheritance laws play a significant role in property ownership. These laws dictate how property is inherited and can affect estate planning. It's important to understand these laws to ensure that property is passed on according to the owner's wishes and legal requirements.

Joint Ownership

Joint ownership, where property is owned by two or more individuals, is common in Malta. Each owner's rights and responsibilities can vary depending on the nature of the ownership agreement. Understanding the legal implications of joint ownership, including rights to sell, lease, or bequeath the property, is essential.

Property Boundary and Easement Laws

Property boundaries and easements are important legal considerations. Easements may grant rights to non-owners for specific uses of the property, such as right of way. Ensuring that property boundaries are clearly defined and understanding any existing easements are crucial to avoid disputes.

Planning and Development Regulations

Property owners must comply with Malta's planning and development regulations. These regulations dictate what can be built or altered on a property and are enforced by the Planning Authority. Compliance with these regulations is key to avoiding legal issues and fines.

Rental Regulations

For investors in rental properties, understanding Malta's rental regulations is vital. These laws cover aspects like rent control, tenant rights, and obligations of landlords. Recent reforms have introduced new rules for rental contracts, aiming to strike a balance between the rights of landlords and tenants.

Environmental Laws and Building Standards

Environmental laws and building standards are increasingly relevant in property ownership. Regulations regarding building safety, energy efficiency, and environmental impact affect property development and maintenance. Adhering to these regulations is not only a legal requirement but also a responsibility towards sustainability.

Title Searches and Property Registration

Conducting title searches and registering property correctly are integral to property ownership. Title searches reveal any encumbrances or liens on the property, while registration ensures legal recognition of ownership. These processes provide legal security and clarity in property transactions.

Restrictions on Property Usage

Certain properties, especially those in protected or historic areas, may have restrictions on how they can be used or altered. Being aware of these restrictions is important to avoid legal complications and preserve the cultural and historical integrity of the property.

Rights of Way and Shared Amenities

In properties with shared amenities or rights of way, understanding and respecting these rights is crucial. This includes shared driveways, walls, or utilities. Navigating these shared rights requires a good understanding of the legal implications and often, cooperation with neighbors or other stakeholders.

Mortgage Regulations and Liens

If a property is purchased with a mortgage, it's important to understand the legal implications, such as the lender's rights and any liens on the property. This understanding is crucial for managing financial obligations and maintaining clear title to the property.

Legal Assistance in Property Rights Issues

Given the complexities of property rights and ownership regulations, seeking legal assistance is advisable. A lawyer specializing in property law can provide valuable guidance, ensuring that your rights are protected and that you comply with all relevant regulations.

Staying Informed on Legal Changes

Laws and regulations governing property rights and ownership can change. Staying informed about these changes is important to ensure ongoing compliance and to make informed decisions about property investment.

Handling Disputes and Legal Conflicts

In case of disputes or legal conflicts regarding property rights, understanding the legal avenues for resolution is important. This includes negotiation, mediation, or legal proceedings, depending on the nature of the dispute.

Understanding property rights and ownership regulations is a key aspect of real estate investment in Malta. These regulations dictate the legal framework within which property transactions occur and define the rights and responsibilities of property owners. Navigating these laws and regulations effectively is crucial for securing your investment and ensuring lawful and hassle-free ownership.

4.5: RESOLVING LEGAL DISPUTES IN REAL ESTATE TRANSACTIONS

Legal disputes in real estate transactions can be complex and challenging. In Malta, as in any jurisdiction, these disputes can arise over issues like breach of contract, property boundaries, ownership rights, or construction problems. Effectively resolving these disputes is essential to protect your investment and interests. This section explores the various mechanisms and strategies for resolving legal disputes in the context of Maltese real estate transactions.

Identifying the Nature of the Dispute

The first step in resolving any legal dispute is to clearly identify the issue. Disputes in real estate can range from minor misunderstandings to significant legal disagreements. Common disputes include disagreements over contract terms, defects in property after purchase, boundary disputes, and issues with property development.

Negotiation and Mediation

Before moving to more formal methods of dispute resolution, negotiation and mediation are often effective first steps. These processes involve discussions between the parties to reach an amicable resolution. Mediation, in particular, involves a neutral third party to facilitate the resolution process.

Utilizing Legal Counsel

Involving legal counsel early in the dispute resolution process is advisable. A lawyer specializing in real estate law can provide valuable advice on your legal rights and options and can represent your interests in negotiations or further legal proceedings.

Arbitration

Arbitration is a form of dispute resolution where a neutral third party, the arbitrator, makes a decision to resolve the dispute. This method is less formal than court proceedings and can be faster and more cost-effective. In Malta, arbitration is often used for real estate disputes, especially those involving construction and development.

Litigation

If negotiation, mediation, and arbitration do not resolve the dispute, litigation may be necessary. This involves taking the dispute to court, where a judge will hear the case and make a legally binding decision. Litigation can be time-consuming and expensive, but it may be necessary for complex or high-stakes disputes.

Contractual Clauses for Dispute Resolution

Many real estate contracts include clauses specifying how disputes will be resolved. These may mandate arbitration or mediation before litigation or may specify the jurisdiction in which disputes will be heard. Understanding these clauses is crucial for knowing your rights and obligations in case of a dispute.

Preventing Disputes through Clear Contracts

One of the best ways to prevent disputes is to ensure that all contracts and agreements are clear, comprehensive, and legally sound. This includes ensuring that all terms are clearly defined, responsibilities are outlined, and any potential areas of conflict are addressed.

Documenting Communications and Agreements

Keeping detailed records of all communications and agreements related to the property transaction can be invaluable in resolving disputes. This documentation can provide clear evidence of the terms agreed upon and actions taken by both parties.

Understanding Statutory Rights and Obligations

Being well-informed about your statutory rights and obligations can prevent disputes and aid in their resolution. This includes understanding laws related to property ownership, sale, and tenancy in Malta.

Resolving Tenant and Landlord Disputes

For investment properties, disputes between landlords and tenants are common. Understanding tenant rights and landlord obligations, often outlined in the rental agreement, is key to resolving these disputes.

Boundary Disputes and Surveys

In case of boundary disputes, conducting a professional survey can help clarify property lines and resolve disagreements. Surveyors can provide an unbiased report on the property boundaries, which can be used as a basis for resolution.

Dealing with Construction Disputes

Disputes related to construction, whether with contractors or developers, require a specific approach. This often involves reviewing the construction contract, assessing the work done, and possibly engaging experts to evaluate the quality of the construction.

Alternative Dispute Resolution (ADR)

ADR methods like mediation and arbitration are increasingly popular in real estate disputes for their efficiency and cost-effectiveness. ADR can often lead to solutions that are mutually agreeable and less adversarial than court proceedings.

Expert Witnesses in Real Estate Disputes

In some cases, expert witnesses may be required to provide testimony on specific aspects of the dispute, such as property valuation, construction standards, or real estate practices in Malta.

Continuous Legal Updates and Advice

Staying informed about changes in real estate laws and regulations can help in both preventing and resolving disputes. Regular legal advice and updates can provide you with the knowledge to handle disputes more effectively.

Resolving legal disputes in real estate transactions requires a strategic approach, combining negotiation, legal knowledge, and, when necessary, formal dispute resolution methods. Whether through amicable settlement or formal proceedings, the aim is to reach a resolution that protects your rights and interests while maintaining the integrity of the property transaction.

CHAPTER 5:
THE BUYING PROCESS IN DETAIL

Embarking on a property purchase, particularly in a distinct market like Malta, involves navigating a series of structured steps. This chapter delves into the detailed buying process, providing a comprehensive guide from the initial property search to the final acquisition. We'll explore the intricacies of making an offer, negotiating terms, understanding the legalities of the Promise of Sale agreement, conducting due diligence, and the finalization of the sale. This thorough walkthrough is designed to equip buyers with essential knowledge and insights, ensuring a smooth and informed journey through each stage of acquiring property in Malta.

5.1: SEARCHING FOR THE RIGHT PROPERTY

The journey to property ownership in Malta starts with the crucial step of finding the right property. This process involves more than just browsing listings; it requires a strategic approach to identify a property that meets your specific needs and investment goals. This section outlines the key considerations and steps involved in searching for the right property in Malta.

Defining Your Criteria

Begin by defining your criteria for the ideal property. Consider factors like location, type of property (such as an apartment, villa, or farmhouse), size, amenities, and your budget. Clarity on these criteria will streamline your search and make it more efficient.

Understanding Different Localities

Malta offers a diverse range of localities, each with its unique characteristics and appeal. From the bustling streets of Valletta to the tranquil surroundings of Gozo, understanding the nuances of different areas is essential. Consider aspects like connectivity, local amenities, safety, and community vibe.

Setting a Realistic Budget

Your budget is a determining factor in your property search. It should account not only for the purchase price but also for additional costs such as taxes, legal fees, and potential renovation expenses. Setting a realistic budget helps in focusing your search on properties you can afford.

Utilizing Online Resources and Real Estate Agents

Leverage online property portals and real estate agencies to aid your search. Online portals offer the convenience of browsing properties at your leisure, while real estate agents provide valuable local insights and can offer access to off-market listings.

Visiting Properties

Physical property visits are crucial. They offer a firsthand view of the property, its condition, and its surroundings. During visits, pay attention to factors like the property's structural condition, natural light, noise levels, and neighborhood.

Assessing Property Potential

When viewing properties, assess their potential. This might involve considering the property's scope for appreciation, rental yield potential, or renovation possibilities. For investment properties, consider the demand and rental rates in the area.

Evaluating New Developments vs. Resale Properties

The choice between new developments and resale properties depends on your preferences and investment goals. New developments offer modern amenities and fewer maintenance issues but might come at a higher price. Resale properties can offer better value and character but may require additional investment in renovations.

Seeking Professional Advice

Consulting with real estate professionals can provide insights that might not be apparent from listings and viewings. Professionals can offer advice on the property's true market value, potential hidden costs, and legal considerations.

Considering Long-term Implications

Consider the long-term implications of your property choice. Think about future marketability, the potential for area development, and how the property fits into your long-term investment or personal goals.

Understanding Legal and Regulatory Framework

Be aware of the legal and regulatory framework surrounding property ownership in Malta. This includes understanding planning regulations, property taxes, and, for foreign buyers, any special acquisition requirements.

Checking Infrastructure and Services

Examine the infrastructure and services available in the area, such as transportation, healthcare, schools, and shopping facilities. The availability and quality of these services can significantly impact your living experience or the property's appeal to potential tenants.

Considering Lifestyle and Personal Preferences

Your lifestyle and personal preferences play a significant role in choosing the right property. Whether you prefer a bustling city life, a quiet village, or coastal living, Malta offers diverse options to match different lifestyles.

Investigating Future Developments

Research any planned developments or changes in the area that could affect the property's value or your quality of life, such as new construction projects, infrastructure developments, or zoning changes.

Patience and Perseverance

Property hunting requires patience and perseverance. It may take time to find the perfect match for your criteria, and it's important not to rush into a decision.

Flexibility in Property Search

While having specific criteria is important, maintaining some level of flexibility can open up more possibilities and might lead you to a property that exceeds your expectations but in a different way.

In searching for the right property in Malta, a thoughtful and well-informed approach is key. By clearly defining your criteria, understanding different localities, setting a realistic budget, and leveraging both online resources and professional advice, you can navigate the property search process effectively. This approach ensures that you not only find a property that meets your requirements but also represents a sound investment or a comfortable home for the future.

5.2: MAKING AN OFFER AND NEGOTIATING TERMS

The process of making an offer and negotiating terms is a critical stage in the property buying journey. It requires not only a good understanding of the property's value but also the skill to navigate negotiations to arrive at a mutually agreeable deal. This section focuses on strategies and considerations for effectively making an offer and negotiating terms in the Maltese property market.

Understanding Market Value

Before making an offer, it's crucial to have a clear understanding of the property's market value. This involves researching recent sales of similar properties in the area and considering factors such as location, size, condition, and amenities. An accurate assessment of the market value serves as a strong foundation for your offer.

Determining Your Offer Price

Your initial offer should reflect both the property's value and your budget. It's common practice to start with an offer below the asking price, leaving room for negotiation. However, the offer should be realistic and respectful, considering market conditions and the seller's position.

Consideration of Seller's Motivation

Understanding the seller's motivation can be advantageous in negotiations. For instance, if the seller is looking to close quickly, they may be more open to a lower offer for a faster sale. Conversely, if the seller isn't in a rush, they may hold out for a higher price.

Effective Communication

Effective communication is key in the negotiation process. Articulate your offer and terms clearly and be open to discussions. Good communication can help build a positive relationship with the seller, which can be beneficial in negotiations.

Negotiating Terms Beyond Price

Negotiations in real estate are not just about the price. They can also involve terms such as the closing date, inclusions or exclusions in the sale (like appliances or furniture), and contingencies like obtaining a mortgage or selling your current home.

Use of Conditional Offers

Conditional offers, based on certain prerequisites being met (such as a satisfactory property inspection or securing financing), are common. These conditions protect you as the buyer but must be used judiciously as too many contingencies may make your offer less attractive.

Seeking Professional Assistance

Having a real estate agent or lawyer during negotiations can be invaluable. Professionals bring experience and knowledge to the process, can provide advice on appropriate offer levels, and can handle negotiations on your behalf.

The Art of Compromise

Successful negotiation often involves compromise. Be prepared to make concessions, but also know your limits and the aspects of the deal that are non-negotiable for you.

Responding to Counteroffers

Be prepared for counteroffers. Evaluate each counteroffer carefully against your budget and market value assessments. Respond in a timely and considered manner to keep the negotiations moving forward.

Understanding Seller's Counterarguments

Listen to the seller's counterarguments and try to understand their perspective. This can provide insights into their priorities and help you adjust your offer or terms accordingly.

Maintaining a Business Perspective

It's important to maintain a business perspective and not let emotions overly influence your decisions. Stay focused on your investment goals and the financial aspects of the transaction.

Being Informed About Legal Aspects

Be well-informed about the legal aspects of the offer and purchase process. Understanding the legal implications of the terms being negotiated is crucial to ensure a smooth transaction.

Patience in Negotiations

Negotiations can take time, and patience is often key. Rushing the process can lead to less favorable terms or even jeopardize the deal.

Walking Away When Necessary

Be prepared to walk away if the terms are not favorable or if the negotiations reach an impasse. It's better to forego a deal than to commit to terms that are not advantageous or beyond your budget.

Finalizing the Negotiated Terms

Once terms are agreed upon, ensure they are accurately reflected in the contract or agreement. This is where legal counsel can assist in reviewing the contract to ensure it aligns with the negotiated terms.

Building a Rapport with the Seller

Building a positive rapport with the seller can facilitate smoother negotiations. A respectful and professional relationship can lead to a more amicable negotiation process.

Making an offer and negotiating terms are critical skills in the property buying process. Understanding the market, communicating effectively, being prepared to compromise, and having professional support are key to successful negotiations. This approach enables you to secure property on terms that align with your investment goals and financial plan.

5.3: THE PROMISE OF SALE AGREEMENT (KONVENJU)

In Malta, the Promise of Sale Agreement, commonly referred to as the Konvenju, is a fundamental component of the property buying process. This legally binding document sets the stage for the final transfer of property and encompasses various crucial details about the transaction. Understanding the intricacies of the Konvenju is vital for both buyers and sellers as it forms the basis of the property transaction.

Nature of the Konvenju

The Konvenju is a preliminary agreement that outlines the conditions under which the sale of a property will take place. It is a commitment from both the buyer and the seller to complete the transaction under agreed-upon terms within a specified timeframe, typically three months.

Key Components of the Konvenju

A typical Konvenju includes details such as the description of the property, the agreed-upon sale price, the deposit amount (usually 10% of the purchase price), and the completion date. It also lists any conditions that must be fulfilled before the final deed is signed, such as obtaining a bank loan, carrying out a property inspection, or securing necessary permits.

Legal Obligations and Binding Nature

The Konvenju is legally binding. Once signed, both parties are legally committed to proceeding with the sale under the terms outlined. If either party defaults, there are legal repercussions. For instance, if the buyer defaults, they may lose their deposit, while the seller might be obliged to return the deposit in double if they fail to honor the agreement.

Due Diligence Period

The period between the signing of the Konvenju and the final deed is typically used for conducting due diligence. This may include a title search to ensure the seller's legal right to sell the property, applying for bank loans, and carrying out any necessary inspections or surveys of the property.

Deposits and Payments

Upon signing the Konvenju, the buyer usually pays a deposit, part of which includes a portion for stamp duty. This deposit is held in escrow by the notary until the completion of the sale. The terms of the deposit and subsequent payments should be clearly outlined in the Konvenju.

Role of the Notary

A notary plays a crucial role in the Konvenju process. They are responsible for drafting the agreement, conducting the due diligence (such as title searches), and ensuring that all legal requirements are met. The notary also registers the Konvenju with the Public Registry.

Conditions and Clauses

The Konvenju may contain specific conditions and clauses that must be satisfied before the sale can be completed. These could include repair works to be carried out by the seller, obtaining planning permissions, or any other condition agreed upon by both parties.

Extensions and Validity

The Konvenju is valid for the period stipulated within it, often three months. If necessary, both parties can agree to extend this period, for example, if the buyer needs more time to secure financing.

Termination of the Agreement

If any of the conditions in the Konvenju are not met, or if either party chooses not to proceed with the sale, the agreement can be terminated. The consequences of termination depend on the terms outlined in the Konvenju and the nature of the default.

Finalizing the Sale

Once all conditions in the Konvenju are satisfied, the final sale can proceed. The notary prepares the final deed of sale, and the balance of the purchase price is paid to the seller. The transfer of property ownership is then officially recorded.

Legal Representation

Both buyers and sellers are advised to seek legal representation when entering into a Konvenju. Legal counsel can ensure that their rights are protected, and the terms of the agreement are clear and fair.

Understanding Legal Terms

Given the legal nature of the Konvenju, it's important for all parties to fully understand the terms and implications. Any queries or uncertainties should be clarified before signing.

Insurance and Protection

Buyers may also consider insurance options to protect their deposit and investment during the period between the Konvenju and the final deed of sale.

Customizing the Konvenju

The Konvenju can be customized to suit the specific needs of the transaction. Tailoring the agreement to address unique aspects of the property or the needs of the buyer and seller can help avoid future disputes.

The Promise of Sale Agreement is a crucial step in the property buying process in Malta. It sets the legal framework for the transaction and outlines the responsibilities and expectations of both parties. Understanding and carefully drafting the Konvenju is essential for a smooth and successful property transfer.

5.4: DUE DILIGENCE AND PROPERTY INSPECTION

Due diligence and property inspection are pivotal steps in the property buying process, providing a comprehensive understanding of the property's condition and legal standing. These processes are integral in ensuring that you make an informed decision, mitigating risks associated with property investment. This section delves into the critical aspects of due diligence and property inspection in Malta.

The Essence of Due Diligence

Due diligence in property transactions involves a thorough investigation into various aspects of the property and the transaction. This process is crucial for uncovering any potential issues that could affect the value or legality of the property.

Legal Due Diligence

Legal due diligence includes verifying the property's title, ensuring there are no legal encumbrances or disputes, and confirming the seller's legal right to sell the property. It also involves checking for any outstanding mortgages, liens, or legal claims against the property.

Verifying Planning Permissions and Compliance

Checking for planning permissions and ensuring compliance with local building regulations are crucial. This includes verifying that any extensions or alterations to the property are legally approved and comply with Malta's building and planning regulations.

Reviewing Contracts and Agreements

Due diligence extends to reviewing all contracts and agreements related to the property. This ensures that there are no unfavorable terms or hidden clauses that could adversely affect your interests.

Financial Due Diligence

Financial due diligence involves assessing the financial aspects of the transaction. This includes understanding the full cost of the purchase, including taxes, fees, and any ongoing expenses like maintenance or community fees.

Property Inspection: A Critical Element

A professional property inspection is an essential component of the due diligence process. It provides an objective assessment of the property's physical condition, identifying any defects or necessary repairs.

Structural Inspection

A structural inspection assesses the integrity of the property's foundation, walls, roof, and other structural elements. This is vital to ensure the property is safe and sound.

Checking for Repairs and Maintenance

The inspection should identify any immediate repair needs or ongoing maintenance issues. This can include checking the condition of plumbing, electrical systems, heating, and cooling systems.

Assessing Renovation Needs

For properties that require renovations, a thorough inspection can help estimate the potential costs and scope of the work needed. This is crucial for budgeting and planning purposes.

Identifying Potential Health and Safety Issues

Inspectors also look for potential health and safety issues, such as mold, asbestos, or other hazardous materials. Addressing these issues is essential for the well-being of occupants.

Environmental Assessments

In some cases, an environmental assessment may be necessary, particularly for properties on sites with potential contamination or other environmental risks.

Using Certified Inspectors

It's important to use certified inspectors who have the expertise and knowledge to conduct thorough property inspections. Their reports can provide valuable insights into the property's condition.

Negotiating Based on Inspection Results

The results of the property inspection can be used as a negotiating tool. If significant issues are uncovered, you may be able to negotiate a lower purchase price or request that the seller makes repairs before the sale.

Ongoing Maintenance and Upkeep

Understanding the property's maintenance history and future upkeep requirements is part of effective due diligence. This informs you about the long-term costs and efforts required to maintain the property.

Importance of Timeliness

Conducting due diligence and property inspection in a timely manner is crucial. Delays in this process can lead to complications or delays in the transaction.

Documenting Findings

Documenting the findings of due diligence and property inspections is essential. This record can be useful for future reference, especially if any issues arise after the purchase.

Professional Assistance

Engaging professionals, such as lawyers, notaries, and inspectors, during the due diligence process is highly recommended. Their expertise can provide peace of mind and ensure that all aspects of the property are thoroughly vetted.

Due diligence and property inspection are critical in the property buying process, offering a safeguard against potential risks and ensuring that you are fully informed about your investment. These steps allow you to proceed with confidence, armed with the knowledge needed to make a sound decision in your property acquisition.

5.5: FINALIZING THE SALE: THE ACT OF COMPLETION

Finalizing the sale, known as the act of completion, is the conclusive step in the property buying process. This phase involves various crucial actions and legal formalities, marking the transfer of ownership from the seller to the buyer. Understanding this final stage is essential for a smooth and successful conclusion to your property transaction in Malta.

Preparation for Completion

Preparation for the act of completion begins well before the actual day. It involves ensuring that all contractual conditions have been met, finalizing mortgage arrangements, and confirming that all necessary funds are available.

Final Property Inspection

A final inspection of the property is advisable. This is to ensure that the property is in the agreed-upon condition and that any required repairs or alterations have been completed.

Review of Legal Documents

Before the completion, a thorough review of all legal documents is essential. This includes the final deed of sale, mortgage documents, and any other agreements related to the transaction.

Transfer of Funds

The transfer of funds is a key component of the completion process. This typically involves transferring the remaining balance of the purchase price, along with any other fees or duties, to the seller or the seller's legal representative.

Payment of Taxes and Fees

The buyer is responsible for paying any applicable taxes and fees, including stamp duty and notarial fees. These payments are often made through the notary handling the transaction.

Signing the Final Deed

The final deed of sale is signed by both the buyer and the seller in the presence of a notary. This document formally transfers ownership of the property and is the legal culmination of the sale process.

Registration of the Deed

After the signing, the notary registers the deed with the Public Registry. This registration is a crucial legal step, officially recording the change in ownership.

Notary's Role

The notary plays a central role in the act of completion. They ensure that all legal requirements are met, oversee the signing of the deed, handle the transfer of funds, and register the transaction.

Verification of Clear Title

Before completion, verifying that the property has a clear title is crucial. This means that there are no outstanding legal issues, liens, or encumbrances that could affect your ownership.

Handling of Mortgage Documentation

If the purchase involves a mortgage, handling the mortgage documentation correctly is crucial. The lender will often require a copy of the signed deed and confirmation of registration.

Utility Transfers and Other Formalities

Arranging for the transfer of utilities and services into the buyer's name is part of the completion process. This includes electricity, water, and any other services associated with the property.

Receipts and Records

Keeping receipts and records of all transactions and payments made during the completion process is important for future reference and for maintaining a clear financial record of the purchase.

Post-Completion Responsibilities

After the completion, the buyer has various responsibilities, such as maintaining the property, paying ongoing taxes and fees, and adhering to any regulations or laws applicable to the property.

Possession and Access to the Property

Once the sale is completed, the buyer gains possession and full access to the property. The seller is responsible for handing over keys and any relevant documents or information about the property.

Resolving Last-Minute Issues

If any last-minute issues or disputes arise during the completion, they must be resolved promptly to avoid delaying the transaction.

Celebrating the Transaction

Finalizing a property sale is a significant accomplishment. Celebrating this milestone acknowledges the effort and resources invested in successfully completing the transaction.

Professional Guidance

Throughout the act of completion, having professional guidance from a lawyer or notary can provide assurance that the process is handled correctly and efficiently.

Finalizing the sale of a property is a multi-faceted process that requires attention to detail and adherence to legal procedures. From preparing for completion to signing the final deed and handling post-completion formalities, each step is integral to ensuring the successful transfer of ownership. With careful planning, thorough review of documents, and professional assistance, the act of completion can be a smooth and rewarding culmination of your property buying journey.

CHAPTER 6: RENTING VS. BUYING IN MALTA

The decision between renting and buying property in Malta is a significant one, encompassing a range of financial, lifestyle, and long-term planning considerations. This chapter delves into the comparative analysis of renting versus buying in the Maltese real estate market. We will explore the advantages and disadvantages of each option, examining factors such as financial implications, flexibility, investment potential, and personal circumstances. By providing a comprehensive overview of both paths, this chapter aims to equip you with the necessary insights to make an informed decision that aligns with your goals, preferences, and future plans in the context of Malta's unique property landscape.

6.1: PROS AND CONS OF BUYING VS. RENTING

When it comes to property decisions in Malta, choosing between buying and renting is more than just a financial consideration; it's a lifestyle choice that impacts your long-term planning. Each option has its advantages and disadvantages, and understanding these can help you make an informed decision that best suits your circumstances.

Pros of Buying Property

1. **Long-Term Investment**: Buying property is often seen as a long-term investment. Real estate generally appreciates over time, offering potential capital gains.

2. **Stability and Security**: Owning a home provides a sense of stability and security, with no risk of eviction or lease termination.

3. **Freedom to Customize**: Homeownership gives you the freedom to modify and decorate your property according to your preferences.

4. **Building Equity**: Each mortgage payment increases your equity in the property, as opposed to rent payments which are an expense without return.

5. **Potential Rental Income**: Owning property in Malta offers the potential to generate income through rentals, especially given the country's vibrant tourism industry.

Cons of Buying Property

1. **Upfront Costs**: Buying a home involves significant upfront costs, including a down payment, closing fees, and taxes.

2. **Maintenance Responsibilities**: Homeowners are responsible for all maintenance, repairs, and renovation costs, which can be substantial.

3. **Less Flexibility**: Selling a property can be time-consuming, making it more difficult to relocate compared to terminating a rental lease.

4. **Market Risk**: Property values can fluctuate due to market conditions, which can impact the value of your investment.

5. **Mortgage Commitments**: Being tied to a mortgage can be a long-term financial burden, requiring steady income and financial planning.

Pros of Renting Property

1. **Flexibility**: Renting offers more flexibility, making it easier to move for job opportunities or personal reasons without the burden of selling a property.

2. **Lower Initial Costs**: Renting typically requires less money upfront than buying, usually just a security deposit and the first month's rent.

3. **No Maintenance Worries**: Maintenance and repairs are generally the landlord's responsibility, reducing the financial burden on tenants.

4. **No Exposure to Real Estate Market Fluctuations**: Renters are not directly affected by property value fluctuations, which can be an advantage in a declining market.

5. **Freedom from Property Taxes**: Tenants are not responsible for paying property taxes, which can be a significant saving.

Cons of Renting Property

1. **No Equity Building**: Rent payments do not contribute to any asset ownership or equity.

2. **Limited Control Over the Property**: Renters have limited freedom to alter or renovate the property.

3. **Uncertainty**: Leases are typically time-bound, and there's always the uncertainty of lease renewal terms and rent increases.

4. **No Long-Term Financial Gain**: While renting may be cheaper in the short term, it doesn't provide the long-term financial benefits of property appreciation.

5. **Dependent on Landlord**: Renters are dependent on the landlord for property maintenance and addressing any issues that arise.

Personal Circumstances and Preferences

The choice between renting and buying depends largely on personal circumstances and preferences. Factors such as financial stability, career plans, family considerations, and lifestyle choices play a significant role in this decision.

Financial Planning and Consultation

Consulting with financial advisors can provide clarity on the financial implications of buying vs. renting. A thorough analysis of your financial situation, future goals, and market conditions is crucial.

Understanding the Maltese Property Market

The Maltese property market has its unique characteristics. Factors like location, property types, and market trends can influence the decision to buy or rent.

Considering Future Goals and Plans

Your future goals and plans should heavily influence your decision. Buying may be more suitable for those looking for a permanent home and long-term investment, while renting may be better for those seeking flexibility and minimal financial commitment.

Evaluating Lifestyle and Convenience

Your lifestyle and convenience should also guide your decision. Consider factors like job stability, willingness to commit to a mortgage, or the desire for mobility and flexibility.

Choosing between buying and renting in Malta requires a balanced consideration of these pros and cons. It's a decision that goes beyond immediate financial implications to encompass broader aspects of your lifestyle, financial goals, and personal preferences. Carefully weighing these factors will help you make a choice that aligns with your long-term objectives and current circumstances.

6.2: LONG-TERM INVESTMENT POTENTIAL OF BUYING

The long-term investment potential of buying property in Malta is a significant consideration for potential homeowners and investors. This aspect of property acquisition involves evaluating the future value and return on investment that property ownership can offer over time. Understanding the long-term investment potential requires an analysis of various market factors and trends.

Capital Appreciation

One of the primary advantages of buying property is the potential for capital appreciation. Historically, real estate values tend to increase over time, which can result in substantial returns when selling the property in the future. Malta's property market has shown resilience and growth, making it an attractive option for long-term capital appreciation.

Rental Income

Buying property in Malta also offers the potential for generating rental income. With its growing tourism industry and appeal as a destination for expatriates and retirees, there is a steady demand for rental properties. Owning a rental property can provide a steady stream of income, contributing to the property's overall return on investment.

Leveraging Property

Property ownership allows for leveraging, where you can use your property as collateral to secure additional financing. This can be a powerful tool for further investment or property development, potentially increasing the property's value and your investment portfolio.

Tax Benefits

Investing in property can offer various tax benefits. These may include deductions for mortgage interest, property taxes, and operating expenses for rental properties. Understanding the specific tax implications and benefits in Malta is crucial for maximizing the investment potential.

Stability in Real Estate Investment

Compared to other investment forms like stocks or bonds, real estate is often considered a more stable investment. The physical asset of property provides a tangible security that can withstand market fluctuations more robustly.

Hedge Against Inflation

Real estate investment is often seen as a hedge against inflation. As the cost of living increases, so typically does the value of property and rental income, helping to protect the purchasing power of your investment.

Building Equity

Buying property enables the building of equity over time. As you pay down the mortgage, your equity – the property's value minus any debts against it – increases, which can be a significant financial resource.

Improvements and Value Addition

Owning property allows you to make improvements or renovations that can increase its value. Strategic enhancements can significantly boost the property's market worth and appeal.

Market Dynamics in Malta

Understanding the dynamics of the Maltese property market is crucial for long-term investment. Factors like economic growth, infrastructure development, and changes in housing policies can impact property values.

Diversification of Investment Portfolio

Real estate can be a valuable part of a diversified investment portfolio. Including property in your investment mix can spread risk and provide a balance to more volatile investments.

Retirement Planning

For many, buying property is a part of retirement planning. Owning your home outright by retirement can reduce living costs and provide financial security. Additionally, property can be a valuable asset to pass on to heirs.

Consideration of Location and Property Type

The long-term investment potential can vary significantly based on location and property type. Properties in prime locations or in areas slated for development typically offer higher appreciation potential.

Professional Appraisal and Market Analysis

Before buying, a professional appraisal and thorough market analysis can provide insights into the property's potential value increase. This analysis should consider current market trends and future projections.

Long-Term Market Trends and Economic Factors

Evaluating long-term market trends and economic factors is key to understanding the investment potential. Factors like population growth, tourism trends, and economic stability play a significant role in the real estate market's performance.

Mitigating Risks

While the potential for long-term gains is significant, it's important to mitigate risks by thoroughly researching the property and market, understanding your financial capability, and planning for market fluctuations.

Exit Strategy

Having an exit strategy is important for real estate investment. Understanding when and how you might sell the property can maximize your returns and align with your overall financial goals.

In summary, the long-term investment potential of buying property in Malta can be substantial, offering opportunities for capital appreciation, rental income, and portfolio diversification. However, it requires careful consideration of market trends, location, property type, and personal financial goals. With the right approach and strategic planning, property investment can provide significant long-term benefits and financial security.

6.3: FLEXIBILITY AND EASE OF RENTING

Renting property in Malta presents a different set of advantages, primarily centered around flexibility and ease. This option is often favored by those who are not ready for the long-term commitment of buying or who require more adaptability in their living arrangements. Understanding the benefits and considerations of renting is crucial for making an informed decision that aligns with personal circumstances and lifestyle preferences.

Flexibility in Location and Mobility

One of the key benefits of renting is the flexibility it offers in terms of location and mobility. Renters can choose to live in different areas, experiencing various lifestyles without the commitment of a long-term investment. This mobility is particularly beneficial for individuals whose jobs require frequent relocation or for those exploring different neighborhoods before deciding where to settle.

No Long-Term Financial Commitment

Renting does not involve a long-term financial commitment like buying a property. This aspect can be particularly appealing for people who are not in a position to make a significant financial investment or who prefer to avoid the responsibilities that come with property ownership.

Lower Initial Financial Outlay

The initial financial outlay for renting is generally lower than buying. Typically, renters are required to pay a security deposit and the first month's rent, which is significantly less than the down payment and additional costs associated with purchasing a property.

Absence of Maintenance Responsibilities

Maintenance and repair responsibilities usually fall on the landlord, relieving renters of these obligations. This can result in significant savings and reduces the hassle of dealing with property upkeep.

Easier to Adapt to Life Changes

Renting offers the ability to adapt more easily to changes in life circumstances, such as changes in family size, job relocations, or alterations in financial status. The ability to move at the end of a lease term, or sometimes even before, provides a level of adaptability that owning a home does not.

No Exposure to Property Market Fluctuations

Renters are not directly exposed to property market fluctuations in the same way homeowners are. This means that in a declining market, renters are not at risk of finding themselves in negative equity, where the value of a property is less than the outstanding balance on the mortgage.

Opportunity to Invest Elsewhere

For those who choose to rent rather than buy, there is the potential to invest the money that would have been used for a property purchase in other ventures. This can include stocks, bonds, or other investment opportunities that might offer higher liquidity or different risk-return profiles.

Short-Term Commitment

Lease agreements are typically short-term, often ranging from one to a few years. This short-term commitment is ideal for individuals who are uncertain about their long-term plans or who anticipate needing to move in the near future.

Access to Amenities

Some rental properties, particularly in apartment complexes, offer access to amenities like pools, gyms, and common areas. These amenities can enhance the living experience without the additional costs of maintenance and upkeep that a homeowner would incur.

Building Credit History

Renting can provide an opportunity to build or improve a credit history. Consistent and timely rent payments can be beneficial for individuals looking to enhance their credit score, which can be helpful in future financial endeavors.

Ease of Downsizing or Upsizing

Renting allows for easier downsizing or upsizing as needs change, without the hassle of selling and buying property. This can be particularly advantageous for individuals or families experiencing life transitions.

Potential for All-Inclusive Payments

Some rental agreements include utilities and other services in the monthly rent, simplifying budgeting and payments. This all-inclusive approach can make financial planning more straightforward for renters.

No Property Taxes or Home Insurance Costs

Renters are not responsible for property taxes or homeowners' insurance, which are typically the responsibility of the landlord. This absence of additional financial burdens is a notable benefit of renting.

Testing the Property Market

Renting offers the opportunity to test the property market and understand different neighborhoods before committing to buying. This can be especially useful for those new to Malta or uncertain about where they want to live.

Networking and Community Benefits

In rental communities, there are often opportunities for networking and community engagement. This can be particularly appealing for those looking to build social connections in a new area.

Renting in Malta offers flexibility, ease, and a lower financial burden compared to buying property. It provides the freedom to move, adapt to life changes, and avoid the responsibilities and risks associated with property ownership. For many, particularly those who value mobility or are in transitional phases of their lives, renting can be a practical and advantageous option.

6.4: UNDERSTANDING RENTAL LAWS AND REGULATIONS

Navigating the rental market in Malta requires a thorough understanding of the local rental laws and regulations. These laws are designed to protect both landlords and tenants and ensure fair and legal rental practices. Being well-informed about these regulations is crucial for anyone involved in renting property, whether as a landlord or a tenant.

Residential Leases Act

The Residential Leases Act, introduced in Malta in recent years, has brought significant changes to the rental market. This Act was designed to provide more security and stability to tenants while ensuring that landlords can benefit fairly from their investments.

Registration of Rental Contracts

One of the key requirements of the new legislation is the mandatory registration of rental contracts with the Housing Authority. This ensures that all rental agreements are recorded, providing a level of transparency and security for both parties.

Minimum and Maximum Lease Terms

The Act sets out minimum and maximum lease terms for residential properties. Short-term leases are defined as those not exceeding six months, while long-term leases must be for a minimum of one year. These stipulations provide stability for tenants and predictability for landlords.

Security Deposits and Rent Increases

The legislation also regulates security deposits and rent increases. Landlords are typically allowed to request a security deposit, which is often equivalent to one month's rent. Rent increases are also regulated, with clear guidelines on how and when they can be implemented.

Notice Periods and Termination of Lease

The Act outlines specific notice periods that must be adhered to by both landlords and tenants when terminating a lease. These periods vary depending on the length of the lease and the reasons for termination, providing a framework for ending rental agreements.

Rights and Obligations of Landlords and Tenants

The legislation clearly defines the rights and obligations of both landlords and tenants. This includes maintenance responsibilities, respect for the tenant's privacy, and adherence to the terms of the rental agreement.

Rent Registration System

The Rent Registration System, implemented as part of the Act, is an online system where landlords must register all residential rental contracts. This system aids in enforcing legal compliance and provides an official record of rental agreements.

Maintenance and Repairs

Rental laws stipulate the responsibilities for maintenance and repairs of the property. Generally, landlords are responsible for major repairs and maintenance, while tenants are responsible for minor repairs and day-to-day maintenance.

Fair Housing and Non-Discrimination

Laws also ensure fair housing and prohibit discrimination based on race, religion, gender, or other factors. Both landlords and tenants must adhere to these non-discrimination policies.

Dispute Resolution

In case of disputes between landlords and tenants, the law provides mechanisms for resolution. This may involve mediation or legal proceedings, depending on the nature of the dispute.

Energy Performance Certificates

Landlords are required to provide Energy Performance Certificates (EPCs) for their rental properties. EPCs give information about a property's energy efficiency and are part of Malta's commitment to environmental sustainability.

Subletting and Assignment of Lease

The laws also cover the rules regarding subletting and assignment of leases. Tenants typically need the landlord's permission to sublet the property or assign the lease to another person.

Property Insurance

While not legally mandated, it is advisable for landlords to have property insurance. Tenants may also consider renter's insurance to protect their personal belongings.

Regular Updates to Legislation

Rental laws and regulations can be subject to changes and updates. Staying informed about current legislation is important for both landlords and tenants to ensure compliance.

Professional Legal Advice

Seeking professional legal advice can be beneficial, especially for complex rental situations or disputes. Legal experts can provide guidance based on the current laws and best practices in the rental market.

Understanding the rental laws and regulations in Malta is essential for navigating the rental market effectively. Whether you are a landlord or a tenant, being informed about your legal rights and responsibilities ensures that rental agreements are fair, legal, and beneficial for both parties. By adhering to these laws, you can foster a positive and lawful rental experience.

6.5: MAKING THE DECISION: RENT OR BUY?

Deciding whether to rent or buy property in Malta is a significant choice that impacts your financial and lifestyle future. This decision should be based on a thorough evaluation of your personal circumstances, financial situation, and long-term goals. This section aims to guide you through the critical factors to consider, helping you make an informed choice that aligns with your objectives.

Assessing Financial Readiness

The first step in making this decision is assessing your financial readiness. Buying a property requires a substantial upfront investment, including a down payment, closing costs, and ongoing expenses like mortgage payments, property taxes, and maintenance costs. Renting, on the other hand, typically involves a lower initial financial commitment and predictable monthly expenses.

Evaluating Market Conditions

Understanding the current real estate market conditions in Malta is crucial. Factors such as property prices, interest rates, rental yields, and market trends can influence whether buying or renting is more advantageous at a given time.

Long-term vs. Short-term Perspective

Consider your long-term and short-term plans. Buying is generally considered a long-term investment and can be beneficial if you plan to stay in the same location for many years. Renting offers more flexibility, making it suitable for those who anticipate relocating or whose circumstances may change in the short to medium term.

Lifestyle Considerations

Your lifestyle preferences and needs play a significant role in this decision. Buying a home offers stability, a sense of belonging, and the freedom to modify the property. Renting offers flexibility, less responsibility for maintenance, and the ability to easily change residences as needed.

Building Equity vs. Investing Elsewhere

Buying a property allows you to build equity over time, which can be a valuable asset. However, if you're not ready to buy, renting can free up capital to invest in other opportunities that might offer higher returns or suit your financial strategy better.

Maintenance and Upkeep Responsibilities

As a homeowner, you are responsible for all maintenance and repairs, which can be costly and time-consuming. As a renter, these responsibilities typically fall to the landlord, offering a hassle-free living experience.

Tax Implications

Consider the tax implications of buying versus renting. Homeownership can offer tax benefits such as deductions on mortgage interest, which can be a significant financial advantage. Renters don't have these benefits but also don't have to pay property taxes.

Future Property Value

Consider the potential for property value appreciation in Malta. If the market is poised for growth, buying could lead to substantial capital gains. However, if the market is unstable or declining, renting might be a safer option.

Risk Tolerance

Buying property involves certain risks, including market fluctuations and the possibility of property devaluation. Your risk tolerance should align with the decision to buy or rent.

Job Security and Mobility

Your job security and the need for mobility are important considerations. If your job requires frequent relocation or if there is uncertainty in your employment, renting can provide the necessary flexibility.

Emotional Factors

Homeownership often carries emotional value, providing a sense of pride and belonging. Evaluate how important these emotional factors are in your decision-making process.

Financial Planning and Future Goals

Align your decision with your overall financial planning and future goals. Whether it's saving for retirement, investing in education, or other long-term goals, your housing choice should complement these plans.

Consulting with Financial Advisors

Consulting with financial advisors can provide valuable insights into the best course of action based on your financial health and investment goals.

Real Estate as an Investment Option

Consider real estate as part of your overall investment portfolio. For some, buying property is a key investment strategy, while for others, diversifying investments beyond real estate is more suitable.

Opportunity Costs

Evaluate the opportunity costs of buying versus renting. Owning a home ties up a significant amount of capital, which could be used for other investments with potentially higher returns.

Readiness for Homeownership

Lastly, assess your readiness for homeownership beyond just financial aspects. Consider if you are prepared for the responsibilities and commitment that owning a home entails.

Making the decision to rent or buy in Malta involves a complex interplay of financial, personal, and lifestyle factors. It's a decision that should be carefully considered, taking into account your current situation and future aspirations. Whether you choose to buy a property as a long-term investment or prefer the flexibility and ease of renting, ensuring that your decision aligns with your overall life strategy is key to making a choice that you are content with for years to come.

CHAPTER 7:
SPECIAL CONSIDERATIONS FOR FOREIGN INVESTORS

Investing in Malta's property market as a foreign investor comes with a unique set of considerations and requirements. This chapter specifically addresses the factors that non-Maltese investors need to be aware of when navigating the local real estate landscape. From understanding the legal framework governing foreign property ownership to exploring investment incentives and navigating tax implications, this chapter provides a comprehensive guide tailored to the needs of foreign investors. It aims to demystify the process, ensuring that foreign investors are well-equipped with the knowledge to make informed decisions and successfully invest in Malta's vibrant property market.

7.1: RESTRICTIONS AND OPPORTUNITIES FOR NON-RESIDENTS

For foreign investors looking at Malta's real estate market, it is important to navigate the balance between restrictions and opportunities that exist for non-residents. Understanding these parameters is essential for a successful investment in Malta.

Acquisition of Immovable Property (AIP) Permit

Non-residents typically require an Acquisition of Immovable Property (AIP) permit to purchase property in Malta. This permit is necessary for certain areas and for specific types of properties. The AIP process involves ensuring that certain conditions, such as minimum investment thresholds, are met. It's designed to regulate foreign ownership in Malta, ensuring that investments align with national interests.

Minimum Property Value Requirements

There are minimum property value requirements for foreign investors, which vary depending on the property type and location. These requirements ensure that foreign investment contributes significantly to the local economy.

Special Designated Areas (SDAs)

Foreign investors should be aware of Special Designated Areas (SDAs) in Malta. In these areas, there are fewer restrictions on foreign buyers, allowing easier acquisition of properties. SDAs often include high-end residential complexes and offer luxurious amenities.

Opportunities in Rental Investment

For foreign investors, the rental market in Malta offers lucrative opportunities. With a robust tourism sector and a growing expatriate community, there is a steady demand for rental properties, providing potentially attractive rental yields.

Residency Programs and Tax Incentives

Malta offers various residency programs that can be appealing to foreign investors. These programs often provide tax incentives and other benefits, making property investment in Malta more attractive. For instance, the Malta Residency and Visa Program (MRVP) offers residency rights to individuals who meet certain investment criteria.

Capital Gains and Rental Income Taxation

Understanding the tax implications of property investment in Malta is crucial. This includes taxes on rental income and capital gains. Malta has double taxation treaties with numerous countries, potentially reducing tax liabilities for foreign investors.

Property Management for Foreign Owners

Foreign investors who are not based in Malta may need to consider property management services. Professional property managers can handle the day-to-day aspects of property ownership, such as maintenance, tenant management, and compliance with local regulations.

Legal Representation and Local Expertise

Engaging with legal professionals who understand the nuances of Maltese property law and the specifics of foreign investment is important. They can assist in navigating the legalities, ensuring compliance, and facilitating a smooth transaction.

Potential for High-End Property Investment

Malta's property market offers potential for high-end property investment, particularly in areas like Sliema, Valletta, and the Three Cities. These areas are popular among foreign investors for their historical significance, lifestyle amenities, and investment potential.

Restrictions on Renting Out Properties

There may be restrictions and regulations on renting out properties purchased in Malta, especially for properties bought under certain residency schemes. It's important to understand these restrictions to ensure compliance with Maltese law.

Understanding Local Market Dynamics

Having a clear understanding of local market dynamics, including supply and demand, price trends, and future development plans, is key for foreign investors. This knowledge aids in making informed investment decisions.

Networking and Building Local Connections

Building a network of local contacts, including real estate agents, legal professionals, and fellow investors can provide valuable insights and support in navigating the Maltese property market.

Consideration of Cultural and Lifestyle Factors

Investing in a foreign market also involves understanding the cultural and lifestyle factors. Familiarity with Maltese culture, lifestyle, and the local community can enhance the investment experience.

Exchange Rate Considerations

Foreign investors should consider the impact of exchange rate fluctuations on their investment, particularly in terms of property purchase costs and repatriation of funds.

Evaluating Long-term Commitment

Investing in foreign real estate is often a long-term commitment. Assessing your long-term investment goals and the potential for sustained returns is crucial.

Future Resale Potential

Considering the future resale potential of the property, including marketability to both local and international buyers, is an important aspect of investment planning.

For non-residents, investing in Malta's property market presents a mix of restrictions and opportunities. Navigating these effectively requires thorough research, an understanding of legal and regulatory frameworks, and often, the assistance of professionals with expertise in Maltese real estate. With the right approach, foreign investors can successfully leverage the opportunities presented by Malta's dynamic property market.

7.2: NAVIGATING THE ACQUISITION OF IMMOVABLE PROPERTY (AIP) PERMIT

For many foreign investors and non-residents, purchasing property in Malta often necessitates navigating the Acquisition of Immovable Property (AIP) permit process. Understanding and successfully navigating this process is essential for a smooth property transaction.

Understanding the AIP Permit

The AIP permit is a regulatory requirement for non-residents who wish to purchase property in Malta. It is designed to regulate foreign ownership of Maltese property, ensuring that such investments align with national policies and interests.

Who Requires an AIP Permit?

Generally, non-Maltese citizens and non-residents need an AIP permit to buy property in Malta. There are exceptions, such as citizens of the European Union (EU) who have resided in Malta continuously for at least five years.

Properties Exempt from the AIP Permit

Properties located in Special Designated Areas (SDAs) are exempt from the AIP permit requirement. SDAs are high-end development zones where foreign investors can purchase property with fewer restrictions, often including luxury apartments and villas.

Application Process

The application process for an AIP permit involves submitting a request to the Maltese Ministry responsible for property transactions. The application must include details about the property, the terms of the purchase, and personal information about the buyer.

Documents Required

The documentation required typically includes a copy of the preliminary agreement (Promise of Sale or Konvenju), proof of funds, a copy of the applicant's passport, and possibly other personal documents. It's crucial to ensure all documents are complete and accurate to avoid delays.

Minimum Property Value Thresholds

There are minimum value thresholds for property purchases by foreign buyers, which vary depending on whether the property is an apartment or a house. These thresholds are set by the Maltese government and are subject to change.

Purpose of Purchase

The intended use of the property must be declared in the application. Properties bought by non-residents are typically intended for personal use as a primary residence, a holiday home, or for rental investment purposes.

Timeframe for Approval

The timeframe for the AIP permit approval can vary. It's important to factor in this time when planning your property purchase, as the sale cannot be completed without this permit.

Legal Compliance

Ensuring legal compliance throughout the application process is crucial. Non-compliance can lead to the rejection of the application or legal complications in the future.

Seeking Professional Assistance

Engaging a lawyer or a professional familiar with the AIP permit process can be highly beneficial. They can assist with the preparation and submission of the application and ensure that all legal requirements are met.

Financial Considerations

Financial readiness must be demonstrated as part of the AIP application. This includes showing proof of funds for both the property purchase and additional costs like taxes and fees.

Renewal and Changes

If circumstances change, such as alterations to the property or its use, it may be necessary to inform the authorities or apply for a new permit.

Understanding Conditions and Restrictions

Being aware of any conditions or restrictions attached to the AIP permit is essential. These may include limitations on renting out the property or selling it within a certain period.

Impact on Residency Status

Purchasing property in Malta can have implications for your residency status, particularly under certain investment or residency programs. Understanding these implications is important for long-term planning.

Resale of AIP Properties

Considerations for the future resale of properties bought under an AIP permit should also be taken into account. There may be specific conditions or requirements for selling such properties to other non-residents.

Navigating the AIP permit process is a key step for foreign investors wishing to purchase property in Malta. It requires a comprehensive understanding of the requirements, a meticulous approach to the application process, and often the guidance of professionals experienced in Maltese property law. Successfully obtaining an AIP permit paves the way for a smooth property acquisition and ensures compliance with Maltese regulations.

7.3: CURRENCY AND EXCHANGE RATE CONSIDERATIONS

For foreign investors looking into the Maltese real estate market, understanding the implications of currency and exchange rate fluctuations is critical. These factors can significantly impact the cost of investment and the returns on it. This section focuses on the key aspects of currency and exchange rate considerations that non-resident investors should keep in mind.

Understanding Currency Exchange Rates

The exchange rate between your home currency and the Euro, which is Malta's official currency, plays a crucial role in international property transactions. Fluctuations in exchange rates can affect the actual cost of the property and the investment return. It's important to monitor exchange rates closely and understand how they can impact your investment.

Impact on Property Prices

When converting your home currency to Euros, even a small fluctuation in exchange rates can lead to a significant difference in the property's price. This factor needs to be considered when budgeting for the property purchase.

Exchange Rate Risks

There is an inherent risk involved in dealing with exchange rates. Unfavorable changes in the exchange rate between the time of agreeing to purchase and completing the transaction can increase the cost in your home currency.

Using Currency Hedging Strategies

To mitigate exchange rate risks, investors can use currency hedging strategies. These might include forward contracts, where you lock in the current exchange rate for a future transaction, or options contracts that provide the right, but not the obligation, to exchange currency at a set rate.

Banking and Money Transfer Services

Choosing the right banking and money transfer services is crucial. Banks and financial institutions offer different exchange rates and transaction fees. It's advisable to shop around for the best rates and lowest fees.

Impact on Rental Income and Repatriation

If you're purchasing a property for rental purposes, currency fluctuations can affect your rental income when converted back to your home currency. Additionally, repatriating funds back to your home country may be subject to exchange rate variations.

Local Financing vs. Financing from Home Country

Consider the pros and cons of financing your property purchase in Malta versus obtaining financing in your home country. Local financing in Euros may avoid exchange rate risks, but financing in your home currency might be more favorable depending on interest rates and exchange rate forecasts.

Tax Implications

Currency fluctuations can also have tax implications, especially when it comes to capital gains or losses upon the sale of the property. Understanding these implications is crucial for effective tax planning.

Long-term Perspective

Having a long-term perspective can mitigate some of the risks associated with exchange rate fluctuations. Property investment is often a long-term endeavor, and exchange rates can fluctuate widely in the short term.

Professional Financial Advice

Seeking professional financial advice is highly recommended. Financial advisors can provide insights into currency risks and strategies to mitigate them.

Budgeting for Fluctuations

Incorporate a buffer in your budget to accommodate potential exchange rate fluctuations. This precaution can help ensure that you remain financially comfortable even if currency values shift unexpectedly.

Understanding Currency Trends

Gaining an understanding of historical currency trends between your home currency and the Euro can provide useful insights for predicting future movements, although past performance is not always indicative of future trends.

Regular Monitoring

Regularly monitor currency markets and economic news, as global economic events can significantly impact exchange rates. Staying informed can help you make timely decisions regarding your investment.

Exchange Rate Guarantees

Some financial institutions or currency exchange services offer exchange rate guarantees for a certain period. These can provide certainty and protection against adverse currency movements.

Diversification of Currency Exposure

Consider diversifying your currency exposure. If you have investments in multiple currencies, it can provide a hedge against fluctuations in any single currency.

Impact on Loan Repayments

If you have a mortgage or loan in a different currency from your rental income or repatriation funds, be aware of how exchange rate changes can affect your loan repayments.

Currency and exchange rate considerations are crucial elements in international property transactions. For foreign investors in Malta, these factors can significantly influence the cost and return on investment. Careful planning, strategic hedging, and staying informed about currency trends can help mitigate risks associated with currency fluctuations, ensuring a more secure and predictable investment outcome.

7.4: RESIDENCY AND VISA IMPLICATIONS OF PROPERTY INVESTMENT

Investing in property in Malta can have significant implications for residency and visa status, especially for non-EU investors. Understanding these implications is crucial for those looking to leverage property investment as a pathway to residency or citizenship in Malta. This section outlines the key residency and visa programs linked to property investment and the various requirements and benefits associated with them.

Malta Permanent Residence Program

The Malta Permanent Residence Program (MPRP) is a popular option for non-EU investors. It allows for the granting of permanent residency to individuals and their families who meet specific investment criteria. This typically includes purchasing or renting property in Malta at a certain value, making a government contribution, and fulfilling other financial requirements.

Malta Individual Investor Program (MIIP)

The MIIP is a citizenship-by-investment program that allows individuals to obtain Maltese citizenship by meeting certain investment thresholds. This includes a significant contribution to the national development fund, investment in government-approved bonds or stocks, and a commitment to either purchase or rent property in Malta for a minimum value and period.

Global Residence Program

The Global Residence Program is designed for non-EU, non-EEA, and non-Swiss nationals. It offers a special tax status and residency rights to individuals who purchase or rent qualifying property in Malta and meet other tax and residency conditions.

Residency Requirements for Property Purchase

For certain residency programs, there are specific requirements related to property purchase. This may include minimum investment thresholds and commitments to retain the property for a certain number of years. Compliance with these requirements is crucial for maintaining residency status.

Visa-Free Travel Benefits

One of the appealing aspects of obtaining residency or citizenship in Malta through property investment is the potential for visa-free travel within the Schengen Area. This offers significant mobility and convenience for investors and their families.

Tax Implications of Residency

Obtaining residency in Malta can have tax implications, particularly regarding income tax, inheritance tax, and property taxes. Understanding these implications is important for effective financial planning.

Renewal and Compliance

Residency programs often require regular renewals and compliance with specific conditions, such as physical presence requirements and maintaining the property investment. Failure to comply can result in the loss of residency status.

Family Inclusion

Many of Malta's residency and citizenship programs allow for the inclusion of family members under the main applicant's application. This typically includes spouses, children, and sometimes dependent parents or grandparents.

Due Diligence Checks

Applicants for residency and citizenship programs undergo rigorous due diligence checks. This includes background checks, verification of source of funds, and other security measures.

Professional Legal Assistance

Navigating the complexities of residency and visa implications of property investment often requires professional legal assistance.

Immigration lawyers can provide valuable guidance and ensure compliance with all legal requirements.

Long-term Commitment

Investing in property for residency or citizenship purposes is a long-term commitment. It's important to consider the long-term implications and responsibilities associated with maintaining this status.

Property Investment Thresholds

Property investment thresholds for residency or citizenship programs are subject to change. Staying informed about current requirements is necessary for compliance and successful application.

Economic Self-Sufficiency

Applicants may need to demonstrate economic self-sufficiency and may be required to have health insurance coverage that is valid in Malta.

Impact on Country of Origin Status

Investors should consider how obtaining residency or citizenship in Malta might impact their status in their country of origin, including potential tax obligations or the need to relinquish their original citizenship.

Property Rental and Residency Programs

For some residency programs, renting a qualifying property in Malta is an alternative to purchasing. The rental investment requirements and conditions vary depending on the specific program.

The residency and visa implications of property investment in Malta offer attractive opportunities for non-residents, but they also come with a set of stringent requirements and commitments. Understanding these programs in detail, staying compliant with the conditions, and seeking professional guidance are key to leveraging property investment for residency or citizenship benefits in Malta. This pathway not only provides a tangible investment in real estate but also opens doors to enhanced mobility, lifestyle, and potential tax advantages.

7.5: CULTURAL AND SOCIAL ADAPTATION FOR FOREIGN INVESTORS

For foreign investors in Malta, understanding and adapting to the local culture and social norms is as crucial as navigating the legal and financial aspects of property investment. This cultural and social adaptation not only enhances the investment experience but also plays a significant role in ensuring a comfortable and enriching stay in Malta. This section explores the various aspects of Maltese culture and society that foreign investors should be aware of to integrate seamlessly into the local community.

Understanding Maltese Culture

Malta boasts a rich cultural heritage, influenced by various civilizations over centuries. Embracing this culture means understanding its history, traditions, and values. The Maltese are known for their hospitality and community-centric lifestyle, which can be a refreshing change for investors coming from more individualistic societies.

Language Adaptation

While Maltese is the national language, English is widely spoken, making communication easier for foreign investors. However, learning some basic Maltese phrases can be beneficial for daily interactions and is often appreciated by locals.

Social Norms and Etiquette

Understanding and respecting local social norms and etiquette is important. This includes basic manners, dress codes, and social customs. For instance, the Maltese place great importance on familial bonds and religious traditions.

Building Local Networks

Building a network within the local community can greatly enhance your experience. Engaging with neighbors, participating in local events, and joining clubs or organizations are effective ways to integrate into Maltese society.

Respecting Religious Traditions

Malta is predominantly Catholic, and religion plays a significant role in daily life. Respecting religious traditions, understanding public holiday customs, and being mindful of religious sensibilities are important for social integration.

Participation in Local Events and Festivities

Participating in local events and festivities can provide deeper insights into Maltese culture. Festas, traditional village feasts, and other cultural events are vibrant expressions of Maltese heritage and community spirit.

Understanding Property Etiquette

In the context of property investment, understanding local etiquette around home ownership and neighborly relations is crucial. This includes respecting noise levels, property boundaries, and communal spaces.

Adapting to Lifestyle Differences

Lifestyle in Malta may differ from what foreign investors are accustomed to. Adapting to these differences, whether it's the pace of life, business hours, or general day-to-day activities, is part of the cultural adaptation process.

Awareness of Business Practices

Being aware of local business practices and customs can aid in smoother transactions and interactions. This includes understanding negotiation styles, business meeting etiquette, and the importance of building personal relationships in business.

Engagement in the Local Economy

Engaging in the local economy, such as shopping at local markets, using local services, and participating in community initiatives, can facilitate cultural integration and contribute to the local community.

Food and Cuisine

Maltese cuisine is a blend of Mediterranean flavors and reflects the island's history. Experiencing local food and dining customs is not only a culinary adventure but also a way to connect with Maltese culture.

Healthcare and Education Systems

Understanding the healthcare and education systems is important, especially for investors planning to reside in Malta for extended periods. Familiarizing yourself with these systems ensures that you and your family can access necessary services comfortably.

Dealing with Culture Shock

Culture shock is natural when adapting to a new environment. Acknowledging and understanding this process can help in adjusting more effectively to life in Malta.

Local Media and Information Sources

Following local media and information sources can keep you informed about societal issues, local news, and events, further aiding in cultural adaptation.

Respecting the Environment

Malta's natural environment is one of its greatest assets. Being mindful of environmental practices and participating in conservation efforts demonstrate respect for the island and its ecosystem.

Legal Rights and Responsibilities

Being aware of your legal rights and responsibilities as a foreign investor and resident is crucial. This includes understanding property laws, tax obligations, and residency requirements.

Openness to Learning and Adapting

An open and adaptable attitude is key to successful cultural and social adaptation. Embracing new experiences and being willing to learn from the local community can enrich your stay in Malta and make your investment journey more rewarding.

Cultural and social adaptation is an essential aspect of the property investment journey for foreign investors in Malta. By embracing the local culture, participating in community life, and respecting social and business norms, investors can not only ensure a pleasant and successful investment experience but also enrich their personal and professional lives in this vibrant Mediterranean country.

CHAPTER 8:
MAXIMIZING PROPERTY VALUE

Maximizing the value of your property investment in Malta is a strategic endeavor that requires insight, foresight, and a keen understanding of the real estate market. This chapter focuses on how to enhance and capitalize on the value of your property. From making savvy improvements and renovations to understanding market trends and effective property management, we delve into various techniques and strategies to increase your property's worth and appeal. Whether you're a long-term investor or planning to sell, this guide offers valuable tips and approaches to ensure your property not only retains its value but also experiences appreciable growth in the dynamic Maltese property market.

8.1: RENOVATION AND REMODELING: ENHANCING PROPERTY VALUE

Renovating and remodeling are effective strategies for enhancing the value of property in Malta. Whether preparing a property for sale or improving it for long-term gain, these enhancements can significantly increase both its market appeal and financial worth. This section outlines key considerations and strategies for renovation and remodeling aimed at maximizing property value.

Assessing the Property's Potential

Start by assessing the property's potential for improvement. Identify areas that need updating or could be more attractive to potential buyers or renters. This might include modernizing outdated features, increasing living space, or improving energy efficiency.

Setting a Budget

Establish a realistic budget for renovations. It's important to balance the cost of remodeling with the potential increase in property value. Overspending on renovations may not necessarily yield a proportionate increase in value, so careful financial planning is essential.

Focusing on High-Value Areas

Invest in areas that typically offer the best return on investment. Kitchens and bathrooms are high-value areas where renovations can significantly impact the property's appeal. Updating these spaces with modern fixtures and finishes can make the property more attractive to potential buyers or renters.

Enhancing Curb Appeal

First impressions matter. Enhancing the property's curb appeal can significantly increase its attractiveness. Simple changes like a fresh coat of paint, landscaping, and decluttering can make a big difference.

Improving Energy Efficiency

Energy efficiency is increasingly important to buyers and renters. Investing in improvements like insulation, energy-efficient windows, and eco-friendly heating and cooling systems can increase the property's value and appeal.

Utilizing Space Effectively

Maximizing the use of space is key. Consider reconfiguring layouts to create open-plan living areas, adding storage solutions, or even converting unused spaces like basements or attics into livable areas.

Quality of Workmanship

Ensure high-quality workmanship in all renovations. Poorly executed remodeling can detract from the property's value. Hiring reputable contractors and using quality materials is crucial.

Staying In Line with Local Market Expectations

Understand the local market and what buyers or renters in Malta are looking for. The renovations should align with market expectations to ensure they add real value to the property.

Obtaining Necessary Permits

Before undertaking any significant renovations, ensure that all necessary permits are obtained. Unauthorized work can lead to legal issues and negatively impact the property's value.

Neutral and Timeless Design Choices

Opt for neutral and timeless design choices that will appeal to a broad audience. Highly personalized or trendy designs might not appeal to all potential buyers or renters.

Smart Home Technology

Incorporating smart home technology can increase a property's appeal. Features like smart thermostats, security systems, and energy-efficient appliances are attractive to modern buyers and renters.

Regular Maintenance

Regular maintenance and minor updates can prevent the need for major renovations in the future and help retain the property's value. Addressing issues promptly avoids more significant problems down the line.

Considering Return on Investment

Every renovation decision should consider the potential return on investment. Research which improvements are most likely to increase the property's value in the Maltese market.

Consulting with Real Estate Professionals

Consulting with real estate professionals can provide insights into the most cost-effective renovations for increasing property value. They can offer advice based on current market trends and buyer preferences.

Documenting Renovations

Keep detailed records and receipts of all renovations. This documentation can be valuable for future valuations or sales, demonstrating the investments made in improving the property.

Marketing the Renovations

When selling or renting the property, highlight the renovations in marketing materials. Detailing the improvements can justify a higher price and attract more interest.

Balancing Aesthetics and Functionality

Renovations should balance aesthetics with functionality. Practical and attractive renovations are more likely to increase the property's overall value and appeal.

Avoiding Overcapitalization

Be cautious of overcapitalization, where the cost of renovations exceeds the added value to the property. Understanding the local market cap is essential to avoid this pitfall.

Renovation and remodeling are powerful tools for enhancing the value of property in Malta. Thoughtful planning, quality execution, and a keen understanding of market trends are key to ensuring that these improvements are both aesthetically pleasing and financially beneficial. By strategically investing in renovations, property owners can significantly boost their property's market value and appeal, making it a more attractive prospect for buyers or renters in the competitive Maltese real estate market.

8.2: THE IMPORTANCE OF LOCATION AND AMENITIES

In the realm of real estate, the adage "location, location, location" holds substantial truth, particularly in Malta's diverse property market. The location of a property and the amenities it offers are pivotal factors that significantly influence its value. This section delves into how location and amenities impact property value and investment potential, and why they should be key considerations in property investment strategies.

The Value of a Prime Location

The location of a property is often its most unchangeable attribute and one that heavily influences its desirability and value. Properties in prime locations such as Valletta, Sliema, and St. Julian's tend to have higher value due to their proximity to business centers, historical significance, and tourist attractions. A prime location typically offers better access to amenities, transport links, and leisure activities, all of which are attractive to potential buyers and renters.

Proximity to Essential Services

The value of a property is also determined by its proximity to essential services like supermarkets, schools, healthcare facilities, and public transport. Properties that offer easy access to these services are generally more sought after and command higher prices.

Impact of Scenic Views and Environment

Properties with scenic views, whether of the Mediterranean Sea, historical landscapes, or urban skylines, tend to have enhanced appeal and value. Additionally, properties in areas with lower pollution levels, more green spaces, and a pleasant environment are increasingly valued for the quality of life they offer.

Amenities and Lifestyle Offerings

The amenities a property offers can significantly impact its value. This includes internal features such as modern fittings, energy-efficient systems, spacious layouts, and external features like parking spaces, swimming pools, and garden areas. Properties in developments that offer communal amenities like gyms, pools, and security services are particularly appealing in Malta's market.

Neighborhood and Community

The character of the neighborhood and the sense of community can also influence property value. Areas with a strong community feel, cultural vibrancy, and safety are highly prized. Gated communities or residential areas with community events and facilities can be especially attractive.

Tourist Appeal and Rental Market

For investment properties, locations with high tourist appeal can be lucrative, particularly in terms of rental income potential. Areas with a steady influx of tourists offer the opportunity for short-term rentals, which can yield higher returns than long-term leases.

Future Development Plans

Understanding the future development plans of an area is crucial. Areas slated for future development or improvement can be excellent investment opportunities, as property values are likely to increase with the development.

Accessibility and Connectivity

Good accessibility and transport connectivity enhance a property's appeal. Properties that are easily accessible by public transportation and are close to major roads and highways tend to be more desirable.

Quiet vs. Bustling Areas

The choice between a quiet, residential area and a bustling, urban location depends on the target market. While some buyers or renters prefer the tranquility of secluded areas, others might value the vibrancy and convenience of a city center location.

Cultural and Historical Significance

Properties in areas of cultural and historical significance, such as Valletta or Mdina, often have a unique appeal. The heritage and architectural beauty of these areas can significantly enhance property value.

School Districts for Family-Oriented Properties

For family-oriented properties, being in a good school district can greatly increase value. Proximity to reputable schools is a major draw for families with children.

Impact of Noise and Pollution

The level of noise and pollution in an area can affect property value. Properties in quieter, cleaner areas are generally more desirable and can command higher prices.

Beachfront and Coastal Properties

In Malta, beachfront and coastal properties are highly sought after for their views and lifestyle offerings. These properties often come at a premium due to their unique location.

The Role of Real Estate Agents

Consulting with real estate agents can provide valuable insights into the best locations and amenities based on current market trends and buyer preferences.

The location and amenities of a property are critical factors in determining its value and appeal in the Maltese property market. Whether for personal use or as an investment, considering these aspects can significantly influence the success of your real estate endeavors. A well-located property with desirable amenities not only provides a pleasant living environment but also holds the promise of appreciating value and investment returns.

8.3: CURRENT TRENDS IN MALTESE PROPERTY DESIGN

The real estate market in Malta is continuously evolving, with current trends in property design reflecting both the island's rich history and modern living demands. These trends not only enhance the aesthetic appeal of properties but also contribute to their functionality and sustainability, impacting their value and desirability. This section examines the prevailing design trends in Maltese properties, highlighting how they cater to contemporary lifestyles while respecting the island's architectural heritage.

Blending Traditional and Modern Elements

A significant trend in Maltese property design is the fusion of traditional architectural elements with modern aesthetics. This includes the incorporation of classic Maltese features such as limestone walls, wooden balconies, and patterned tiles, combined with sleek, contemporary finishes. This blend honors Malta's architectural history while meeting the demands of modern living.

Sustainability and Eco-Friendly Design

Sustainability is increasingly at the forefront of property design in Malta. Eco-friendly design elements, such as solar panels, energy-efficient appliances, and water conservation systems, are becoming more prevalent. These features not only reduce the environmental impact but also offer long-term cost savings for property owners.

Maximizing Natural Light

Making the most of Malta's abundant natural light is a key design trend. Large windows, glass doors, and strategically placed skylights are common design features that help create bright, airy spaces while reducing the need for artificial lighting.

Open Plan Living

Open plan living spaces are highly sought after, reflecting a preference for more fluid, versatile living areas. These designs often feature large, open kitchens and living areas that flow seamlessly together, ideal for socializing and family living.

Outdoor Living Spaces

Given Malta's Mediterranean climate, there is a strong emphasis on outdoor living spaces. Properties often feature expansive terraces, rooftop gardens, and private pools, providing a seamless transition between indoor and outdoor living.

Smart Home Technology

The integration of smart home technology is a growing trend. Automated systems for lighting, heating, security, and entertainment are increasingly being incorporated into Maltese homes, offering convenience and enhanced living experiences.

Minimalist and Neutral Interiors

Minimalist designs with neutral color palettes are popular, reflecting a desire for uncluttered, calming living spaces. This style complements the natural beauty of the surrounding landscapes and the traditional Maltese architecture.

Luxury and High-End Finishes

The luxury segment of the Maltese property market sees a trend towards high-end finishes and bespoke fittings. This includes designer kitchens, spa-like bathrooms, and custom-built features, appealing to the discerning buyer.

Adaptability and Multi-Functional Spaces

Designs that offer adaptability and multi-functionality are in demand. This includes rooms that can serve multiple purposes, such as home offices or guest rooms, reflecting the changing needs of homeowners.

Historical Preservation

There is a growing appreciation for preserving historical properties. Renovations of traditional Maltese townhouses and farmhouses, respecting their original character while updating them for modern comfort, are becoming increasingly popular.

Green and Community Spaces

In larger residential developments, there is a trend towards including green spaces and communal areas. These features provide residents with shared outdoor spaces for relaxation and social interaction.

Use of Local Materials

Using local materials in construction and design is a trend that supports sustainability and preserves the local character. This includes the use of Maltese limestone, known for its durability and natural beauty.

Compact and Efficient Layouts

In response to urbanization and limited space, there is a trend towards more compact and efficient layouts. These designs make intelligent use of space, providing functionality without compromising on comfort.

Incorporating Art and Cultural Elements

Incorporating art and cultural elements into property design is a way of celebrating Malta's rich cultural heritage. This can include artworks, artisanal crafts, and custom pieces that reflect Maltese history and traditions.

Focus on Wellness and Health

Designs that focus on wellness and health are becoming more prevalent. This includes incorporating elements like indoor gardens, natural ventilation, and spaces for exercise and relaxation.

Current trends in Maltese property design reflect a blend of traditional and modern elements, with an increasing focus on sustainability, functionality, and aesthetic appeal. These trends are shaping the way properties are being designed and renovated, enhancing their value and appeal in a competitive market. For investors and homeowners alike, staying abreast of these trends is key to ensuring that properties not only meet contemporary standards but also stand out in Malta's dynamic real estate landscape.

8.4: SUSTAINABLE AND ECO-FRIENDLY PROPERTY INVESTMENTS

The trend towards sustainable and eco-friendly property investments is gaining significant momentum in Malta. This shift is driven not only by a growing global consciousness about environmental impact but also by the practical benefits and long-term savings these investments offer. Eco-friendly properties are increasingly viewed as a smart investment, combining environmental responsibility with economic efficiency. This section explores the key aspects of sustainable property investments, highlighting how they can be both a viable and ethical choice in the Maltese property market.

Energy Efficiency in Buildings

Energy efficiency is at the heart of sustainable property investments. Properties designed with energy-efficient features, such as enhanced insulation, energy-saving windows, and efficient heating and cooling systems, consume less energy. This leads to lower utility bills, making these properties more attractive to buyers and renters who are increasingly cost-conscious about energy usage.

Renewable Energy Sources

The integration of renewable energy sources, like solar panels, is becoming increasingly common in Maltese properties. Investing in solar energy not only reduces dependence on traditional energy sources but also offers potential financial incentives, such as feed-in tariffs or tax benefits.

Water Conservation Measures

Water conservation is crucial, particularly in Malta's dry climate. Features like rainwater harvesting systems, water-efficient appliances, and fixtures, and drought-resistant landscaping can significantly reduce water usage and costs.

Use of Sustainable Materials

Sustainable property investment also involves the use of eco-friendly building materials. These materials are typically sourced sustainably, have lower environmental impacts, and can improve indoor air quality. Examples include recycled or renewable materials, non-toxic paints, and locally sourced stone.

Green Building Certifications

Properties that adhere to green building standards and achieve certifications like LEED or BREEAM are highly valued. These certifications are internationally recognized indicators of sustainability and can significantly enhance a property's marketability and value.

Smart Home Technologies

Smart home technologies play a vital role in sustainable properties. Systems that automate lighting, heating, cooling, and irrigation contribute to energy efficiency and offer the convenience of remote management.

Thermal Comfort and Natural Ventilation

Design features that enhance thermal comfort and promote natural ventilation are important in sustainable properties. These features reduce the need for artificial heating and cooling, contributing to a building's energy efficiency.

Land Use and Biodiversity

Sustainable property investments consider the impact of development on land use and biodiversity. This includes preserving natural habitats, using landscaping that supports local flora and fauna, and minimizing land disruption during construction.

Long-Term Cost Savings

Eco-friendly properties often result in significant long-term cost savings. Reduced energy and water bills, lower maintenance costs, and potential tax incentives make these investments economically attractive.

Market Demand for Sustainable Properties

There is a growing market demand for sustainable and eco-friendly properties. Environmentally conscious buyers and renters are increasingly seeking out properties that align with their values, driving demand in this sector.

Impact on Health and Wellbeing

Sustainable properties often offer better indoor air quality and a healthier living environment. Features like natural lighting, non-toxic materials, and improved air circulation contribute to the occupants' health and wellbeing.

Adaptation to Climate Change

Investing in sustainable properties is also a response to climate change. Features like robust insulation and efficient heating and cooling systems make buildings more resilient to temperature variations.

Financial Incentives and Subsidies

Governments and local authorities often provide financial incentives and subsidies for sustainable property investments. These can include tax breaks, grants, or rebates for installing energy-efficient systems or using sustainable materials.

Community and Social Responsibility

Sustainable property investment reflects a commitment to community and social responsibility. By investing in eco-friendly properties, investors contribute to the creation of sustainable communities and the overall reduction of environmental impact.

Potential for Innovation

The sustainable property sector offers potential for innovation in design, construction, and technology. Investors have the opportunity to be part of cutting-edge developments that set new standards in sustainable living.

Risk Mitigation

Sustainable properties can mitigate risks associated with environmental regulations and energy price volatility. Investing in eco-friendly features can future-proof properties against these risks.

Educating Tenants and Buyers

Part of sustainable property investment involves educating tenants and buyers about the benefits and features of eco-friendly living. This education can enhance the value perception of the property.

Sustainable and eco-friendly property investments represent a forward-thinking approach in the real estate market, aligning environmental stewardship with economic practicality. In Malta, where the balance between development and environmental conservation is particularly crucial, these investments offer a pathway to achieving both profitability and sustainability. By focusing on energy efficiency, renewable energy, water conservation, and sustainable materials, investors can contribute positively to the environment while reaping the benefits of an increasingly eco-conscious property market.

8.5: MARKETING YOUR PROPERTY EFFECTIVELY

Marketing a property effectively is a crucial component of the real estate process, particularly in a competitive market like Malta. A well-executed marketing strategy can significantly enhance the visibility of your property, attract the right audience, and ultimately, secure a successful sale or rental. This section explores the various strategies and tools you can employ to market your Maltese property effectively.

Understanding Your Target Market

The first step in effective property marketing is identifying your target market. Is your property more suited to families, young professionals, retirees, or tourists? Understanding the demographics and preferences of your potential buyers or renters is key to tailoring your marketing approach.

Professional Photography and Videography

High-quality visuals are essential in property marketing. Professional photography and videography can showcase your property in the best light, highlighting key features and giving potential buyers or renters a comprehensive view of the property.

Compelling Property Descriptions

Crafting a compelling and detailed description of your property is important. Highlight unique features, benefits, and any recent renovations or upgrades. Use descriptive language to paint a picture of what living in the property would be like.

Online Marketing Platforms

Utilize online marketing platforms effectively. This includes property listing websites, social media channels, and real estate portals. A strong online presence can significantly increase your property's exposure.

Virtual Tours and 3D Walkthroughs

Offering virtual tours or 3D walkthroughs can be particularly effective, especially for attracting international buyers or those who cannot visit the property in person. These tools provide an immersive experience of the property.

Leveraging Social Media

Social media platforms can be powerful tools for property marketing. Platforms like Facebook, Instagram, and LinkedIn can help reach a wide audience. Regular posts, targeted ads, and engaging content can draw attention to your property.

Real Estate Agent Collaboration

Collaborating with experienced real estate agents can enhance your marketing efforts. Agents can provide valuable market insights, access to broader networks, and expertise in selling or renting properties in Malta.

Traditional Marketing Methods

Don't overlook traditional marketing methods. This can include newspaper listings, property brochures, or open house events. A combination of traditional and digital marketing strategies can be effective.

Word-of-Mouth and Networking

Word-of-mouth remains a powerful marketing tool. Leverage your personal and professional networks to spread the word about your property. Networking events and community groups can also be platforms to market your property.

SEO and Online Advertising

Invest in Search Engine Optimization (SEO) for your property listings to ensure they rank higher in search engine results. Online advertising, such as Google Ads or Facebook Ads, can also be used to target specific demographics.

Responsive Communication

Be responsive to inquiries. Prompt and professional communication with interested parties can make a significant difference in marketing your property.

Staging the Property

Consider staging the property to make it more appealing. A well-staged property can help potential buyers or renters envision themselves living there, which can be influential in their decision-making process.

Feedback and Adjustments

Be open to feedback from viewings and adjust your marketing strategy accordingly. If certain aspects of the property are consistently receiving negative feedback, consider addressing these issues.

Utilizing Email Marketing

Email marketing can be an effective way to reach potential buyers or renters. A well-structured email campaign can keep your property top of mind among your contacts.

Market Analysis and Pricing Strategy

Conduct a thorough market analysis to set a competitive price for your property. An attractive pricing strategy can make your property more appealing to potential buyers or renters.

Local and International Markets

Tailor your marketing approach to both local and international markets. For international buyers, highlight the benefits of investing in Malta and provide information about the local lifestyle and amenities.

Highlighting Community and Lifestyle

In addition to the property itself, highlight the surrounding community and lifestyle. Showcase local attractions, amenities, and the overall appeal of living in the area.

Consistent Branding and Presentation

Ensure consistent branding and presentation across all marketing materials and platforms. This creates a professional image and makes your property more recognizable.

Utilizing Analytics

Use analytics tools to track the performance of your online marketing efforts. Understanding which strategies are most effective can help you refine your approach.

Effectively marketing your property in Malta requires a multifaceted approach, combining a deep understanding of your target market with the strategic use of both digital and traditional marketing tools. High-quality visuals, compelling descriptions, responsive communication, and a well-thought-out pricing strategy are key components of successful property marketing. By adopting these strategies, you can enhance your property's visibility, attract the right audience, and increase your chances of a successful sale or rental.

CHAPTER 9:
THE ROLE OF TECHNOLOGY IN REAL ESTATE

In today's fast-paced world, technology plays an increasingly crucial role in the real estate sector. This chapter delves into how technological advancements are revolutionizing the way we buy, sell, manage, and interact with property. From virtual property tours and AI-driven market analyses to blockchain in property transactions and smart home automation, technology is reshaping the landscape of real estate in Malta and beyond. We explore the various technological tools and innovations that are enhancing efficiency, transparency, and convenience in real estate, offering insights into how both investors and homeowners can leverage these advancements to their advantage.

9.1: ONLINE PLATFORMS AND DIGITAL TOOLS FOR PROPERTY SEARCH

The evolution of online platforms and digital tools has transformed the property search process, making it more accessible, efficient, and user-friendly. In Malta, as in many parts of the world, these technological advancements are redefining how buyers and renters explore real estate options. This section explores the array of digital tools available for property search and how they are changing the landscape of real estate hunting.

Property Listing Websites

Property listing websites are the cornerstone of digital real estate searches. These platforms offer extensive listings of properties for sale and rent, complete with photos, descriptions, and contact information. Advanced search filters allow users to refine their search based on location, price, property type, and more. Websites often feature user-friendly interfaces and are regularly updated, providing a comprehensive and current overview of the market.

Mobile Apps for Real Estate

Mobile apps dedicated to real estate bring the convenience of property searching directly to smartphones and tablets. These apps often provide features like push notifications for new listings, GPS-based search functionality, and the ability to save favorite properties, enhancing the property search experience.

Virtual Tours and 3D Walkthroughs

Virtual tours and 3D walkthroughs have become increasingly popular, allowing potential buyers and renters to explore properties remotely. These tools are particularly useful for international clients or those unable to visit properties in person. They provide a realistic view of the property, helping users to visualize the space and layout.

Augmented Reality (AR) and Virtual Reality (VR)

AR and VR technologies are taking property viewing to the next level. Potential buyers can virtually furnish properties, view renovations, or see unbuilt properties in their actual location, providing a more interactive and immersive experience.

Online Marketplaces and Portals

Online marketplaces and real estate portals aggregate listings from multiple sources, offering a broad perspective of the market. These platforms can include user reviews and ratings, adding an additional layer of information for potential buyers or renters.

Social Media Platforms

Social media platforms are emerging as a significant avenue for real estate marketing and search. Realtors and property owners use these platforms to showcase properties, post updates, and interact with potential clients. For buyers and renters, social media offers a more informal way to explore the market and connect with sellers.

Big Data and AI in Property Search

Big Data and Artificial Intelligence (AI) are transforming property searches by analyzing vast amounts of data to provide personalized recommendations and market insights. AI algorithms can predict market trends, suggest properties based on user preferences, and even assess investment potential.

Online Mortgage and Financing Tools

Online tools for mortgage calculation and financing options facilitate the financial aspect of property buying. These tools help users understand their budget, compare mortgage rates, and even apply for loans online, streamlining the financing process.

Online Customer Service and Support

Many real estate platforms offer online customer service and support, providing assistance and answering queries through chatbots or live chat options. This ensures that users receive timely information and guidance throughout their property search.

E-Signatures and Digital Documentation

The use of e-signatures and digital documentation is simplifying the paperwork involved in real estate transactions. These tools enable secure and efficient document signing and sharing, accelerating the process of agreements and contracts.

Crowdsourcing and Community Feedback

Online platforms often allow for crowdsourcing information and community feedback. Users can gain insights from reviews, experiences, and advice shared by others, aiding in making informed decisions.

Geolocation Services

Geolocation services integrated into online platforms enable users to search for properties based on their current location or desired areas. This feature is especially useful for those unfamiliar with the region or exploring new neighborhoods.

Real Estate Blogs and Online Resources

Blogs, forums, and online resources provide additional information on market trends, buying tips, and property management. These platforms offer educational content that can help buyers and renters make informed decisions.

Online Analytics and Reporting Tools

Analytics and reporting tools available on some platforms provide data on property views, market trends, and user engagement. These insights can be valuable for sellers and agents in understanding the market dynamics and refining their marketing strategies.

Integration with Property Management Tools

For investors, some platforms integrate with property management tools, offering features like tenant screening, rent collection, and maintenance requests, streamlining the management of rental properties.

Customizable Alerts and Notifications

Users can set up customizable alerts and notifications for new listings that match their criteria, ensuring they don't miss potential opportunities in a fast-moving market.

Online platforms and digital tools have significantly enhanced the property search process, offering convenience, efficiency, and a wealth of information. From comprehensive property listings to immersive virtual tours, these technologies provide users with the resources needed to navigate the real estate market effectively. As these tools continue to evolve, they are expected to further streamline and personalize the property search experience, making it easier for buyers and renters to find their ideal property in Malta.

9.2: THE IMPACT OF VIRTUAL REALITY IN REAL ESTATE VIEWING

Virtual Reality (VR) is rapidly transforming the landscape of real estate viewing, offering an innovative, immersive experience that transcends traditional property showcasing methods. In Malta, as in the global real estate market, the impact of VR technology is profound, reshaping how properties are presented, viewed, and experienced by prospective buyers and renters. This section delves into the various facets of VR in real estate and its significant implications for the industry.

Enhanced Property Viewing Experience

VR technology enables a 360-degree viewing experience, allowing prospective buyers and renters to explore properties virtually. This immersive experience goes beyond photos and videos, giving a realistic sense of space, layout, and design. VR viewings are particularly advantageous for off-plan properties or those under construction, as they provide a virtual representation of the finished product.

Remote Viewing Capabilities

One of the most significant impacts of VR is its ability to facilitate remote property viewings. This is especially beneficial in the context of international or out-of-town buyers who cannot physically visit the properties. VR technology allows them to tour properties from anywhere in the world, saving time and resources.

Reducing the Need for Physical Viewings

With VR, the need for multiple physical viewings can be significantly reduced. Prospective buyers can shortlist properties more effectively after experiencing them virtually, leading to more focused and fewer physical viewings.

Customization and Personalization

VR technology offers the potential for customization and personalization of property viewings. Users can change aspects like wall colors, furniture layouts, and lighting in a virtual environment, helping them visualize the property as per their preferences.

Attracting Tech-Savvy Buyers

As the real estate market sees an influx of tech-savvy millennials and digital natives, VR viewings align well with their preferences. This technology appeals to a demographic that values innovation and efficiency in their buying journey.

Time and Cost Efficiency

VR viewings are time and cost-efficient for both real estate agents and clients. They minimize the need for travel and scheduling, allowing for a more streamlined viewing process.

Competitive Advantage for Sellers and Agents

Real estate agents and sellers who utilize VR technology gain a competitive edge in the market. Offering VR viewings can make property listings stand out and attract more interest and engagement.

Impact on Property Marketing

VR has revolutionized property marketing strategies. It allows for innovative marketing campaigns that can reach a broader audience, offering a more engaging and interactive way to showcase properties.

Accuracy of Property Representation

VR provides an accurate representation of properties, reducing the gap between expectation and reality often experienced in traditional viewings. This accuracy can help in building trust and transparency in the real estate process.

Interactive and Engaging Viewings

VR viewings are interactive and engaging, offering a dynamic way to explore properties. This interactivity can lead to a more memorable viewing experience and stronger engagement from potential buyers.

Facilitating Architectural Visualization

For architects and developers, VR is a valuable tool for architectural visualization. It allows them to present their designs and concepts in a realistic manner, facilitating better communication of their vision.

Overcoming Geographical Barriers

VR technology overcomes geographical barriers, enabling global reach for property listings. This can open up new markets and opportunities for sellers and agents.

Potential in Property Development and Staging

VR is also used in property development and staging, enabling developers and stagers to create virtual models of properties. This can aid in decision-making regarding design and development before any physical work begins.

Enhancing the Decision-Making Process

VR viewings enhance the decision-making process for buyers and renters. By providing a comprehensive and immersive view of properties, it aids in making more informed and confident decisions.

Challenges and Limitations

While VR technology offers numerous benefits, it also comes with challenges. The cost of VR equipment and the need for technical expertise can be barriers. Additionally, the technology might not yet be widespread among all demographics, limiting its reach.

Future Developments in VR Technology

The future of VR in real estate looks promising, with ongoing advancements expected to further enhance its capabilities and accessibility. These developments could include more realistic and interactive VR experiences and integration with other technologies like AI.

Training and Adoption in the Real Estate Industry

For effective implementation, training and adoption of VR technology within the real estate industry are crucial. Real estate professionals need to be equipped with the skills and knowledge to utilize this technology effectively.

Enhancing Global Real Estate Transactions

VR technology has the potential to enhance global real estate transactions, making it easier for international investors and buyers to explore and invest in properties worldwide.

Virtual Reality is revolutionizing the way properties are viewed and experienced in the real estate market. Its ability to provide immersive, accurate, and remote viewings is not only enhancing the buyer's journey but also offering new avenues for marketing and showcasing properties. As the technology continues to evolve and become more accessible, its impact on the real estate industry is poised to grow, offering exciting possibilities for buyers, sellers,

9.3: UTILIZING BIG DATA FOR MARKET ANALYSIS

In the realm of real estate, big data has become an invaluable asset for market analysis, offering a comprehensive and nuanced understanding of market trends, consumer behavior, and investment opportunities. The application of big data in the Maltese property market, as in other parts of the world, is reshaping how investors, realtors, and stakeholders make informed decisions. This section delves into the role of big data in real estate market analysis and how it is leveraged to gain insights, predict trends, and drive strategic decisions.

Understanding Big Data in Real Estate

Big data in real estate refers to the large volume of data collected from various sources related to property transactions, market trends, consumer preferences, and economic indicators. This data is analyzed to uncover patterns, correlations, and insights that are not discernible through traditional data analysis methods.

Sources of Big Data in Real Estate

Data sources in real estate include property listings, sales records, rental data, demographic information, economic indicators, and even social media trends. These sources provide a wealth of information that can be mined for valuable insights.

Predictive Analysis for Market Trends

Big data enables predictive analysis, where historical and current data are used to forecast future market trends. This can include predicting property price movements, identifying emerging hotspots, or anticipating changes in consumer demand.

Consumer Behavior Insights

Analyzing big data helps in understanding consumer behavior and preferences. Patterns in property searches, purchasing behaviors, and preferred amenities can be identified, allowing for targeted marketing strategies and more customer-focused service.

Enhancing Property Valuation Models

Big data significantly enhances property valuation models. By incorporating a wide range of variables, these models become more accurate and reflective of the current market conditions, leading to more precise property appraisals.

Risk Assessment and Management

Big data aids in risk assessment and management. By analyzing market trends and economic indicators, investors can identify potential risks and make more informed decisions about where and when to invest.

Geospatial Data Analysis

Geospatial data analysis, another facet of big data, involves examining geographical and spatial factors in real estate. This includes analyzing the impact of location, proximity to amenities, and neighborhood characteristics on property values.

Optimizing Investment Portfolios

Investors can use big data to optimize their property portfolios. By understanding market trends and consumer demands, they can strategically invest in properties that are likely to yield high returns or appreciate in value.

Identifying Market Gaps and Opportunities

Big data analysis helps in identifying gaps in the market and untapped opportunities. This could involve finding underserved areas, emerging markets, or new consumer segments.

Improving Marketing and Sales Strategies

Big data informs more effective marketing and sales strategies. By understanding what drives consumer decisions, realtors can tailor their marketing efforts and sales pitches to resonate more strongly with their target audience.

Facilitating Urban Planning and Development

On a larger scale, big data plays a crucial role in urban planning and development. Data-driven insights can guide the development of infrastructure, amenities, and services to meet the needs of the population.

Customizing Client Services

Realtors and property managers can use big data to offer customized services to clients. Insights from data analysis can inform personalized recommendations, tailored property selections, and more efficient client interactions.

Enhancing Real Estate Websites and Apps

Real estate websites and apps can utilize big data to enhance user experience. Features like personalized property recommendations, interactive maps, and market trend analyses can be integrated based on user data and preferences.

Real-Time Market Analysis

Big data enables real-time market analysis, allowing for immediate responses to market changes. This agility is crucial in the fast-paced real estate market, where timing can significantly impact investment success.

Challenges in Utilizing Big Data

While big data offers numerous benefits, there are challenges in its utilization. These include data privacy concerns, the need for advanced analytical tools and expertise, and ensuring data accuracy and relevance.

Future of Big Data in Real Estate

The future of big data in real estate looks promising, with advancements in AI and machine learning expected to further enhance data analysis capabilities. This will likely lead to even more sophisticated market predictions and personalized real estate services.

Collaboration and Data Sharing

Collaboration and data sharing among real estate professionals, government agencies, and developers can amplify the benefits of big data. A collective approach to data analysis can provide a more comprehensive view of the market.

Big data has become an integral part of market analysis in the real estate sector, offering deep insights and aiding in informed decision-making. In Malta's property market, as in global markets, leveraging big data effectively can lead to more strategic investments, better understanding of consumer needs, and ultimately, more successful real estate transactions. As technology continues to evolve, the role of big data in real estate is set to become even more pivotal, transforming how the industry operates and evolves.

9.4: THE ROLE OF SOCIAL MEDIA IN REAL ESTATE MARKETING

Social media has become an indispensable tool in real estate marketing, revolutionizing how properties are marketed and how realtors, buyers, and sellers connect. In today's digital age, platforms like Facebook, Instagram, LinkedIn, and Twitter offer powerful avenues to reach and engage with a wide audience. This section delves into the multifaceted role of social media in real estate marketing and how it's shaping the industry in Malta and beyond.

Building Brand and Presence

Social media allows realtors and property companies to build a brand and online presence. By consistently posting quality content, engaging with followers, and showcasing expertise, real estate professionals can establish themselves as trusted authorities in the industry.

Showcasing Properties

Social media platforms are excellent for showcasing properties. High-quality images, videos, and virtual tours shared on these platforms can reach a vast audience, providing greater exposure than traditional marketing methods.

Targeted Advertising

Social media platforms offer sophisticated targeted advertising options. Realtors can use these tools to reach specific demographics based on interests, location, age, and more. This targeted approach ensures that property listings are seen by potential buyers or renters who are most likely to be interested.

Engaging with Potential Clients

Social media facilitates direct engagement with potential clients. Realtors can respond to queries, participate in conversations, and gather feedback, creating a more personal connection with their audience.

Creating a Community

Through social media, realtors can create and nurture a community of followers interested in real estate. This community can be a valuable resource for sharing market insights, property tips, and industry news, fostering a sense of connection and trust.

Leveraging User-Generated Content

User-generated content, such as reviews, testimonials, and shared experiences, can be leveraged on social media. This content adds credibility and can be persuasive in the decision-making process of potential buyers or renters.

Utilizing Video and Live Streaming

Videos and live streaming are highly effective on social media. Realtors can use these tools for virtual open houses, live Q&A sessions, and property walkthroughs, providing an interactive experience to the audience.

Influencer Collaborations

Collaborating with influencers or local celebrities on social media can amplify property exposure. Influencers can bring their audience and credibility to a property or real estate brand, reaching a broader and more diverse audience.

Market Trends and Insights

Social media is a valuable source of market trends and consumer insights. Realtors can gather information on what buyers are looking for, preferred property features, and emerging real estate trends.

SEO Benefits

Active social media presence contributes to Search Engine Optimization (SEO). Regular posts and user engagement can drive more traffic to real estate websites, improving their search engine ranking.

Cost-Effective Marketing

Compared to traditional marketing methods, social media marketing is relatively cost-effective. Even paid advertising options on social media platforms are generally more affordable and offer better ROI.

Real-Time Marketing and Feedback

Social media allows for real-time marketing and instant feedback. Realtors can quickly gauge the response to their listings and adjust their strategies accordingly.

Mobile Accessibility

With the increasing use of smartphones, social media platforms offer the advantage of mobile accessibility. Users can view property listings, interact with realtors, and stay updated on the go.

Sharing Educational Content

Realtors can use social media to share educational content related to real estate. This can include buying tips, property maintenance advice, and market analyses, positioning them as knowledgeable professionals in the field.

Networking and Collaboration

Social media enables networking and collaboration opportunities within the real estate industry. Realtors can connect with peers, share experiences, and learn from each other, fostering a collaborative environment.

Impact on International Buyers

For international buyers, social media provides an accessible platform to explore properties in Malta. It bridges geographical barriers, allowing for global exposure of local properties.

Sensitivity to Market Changes

Social media marketing strategies must be sensitive to market changes and global events. Strategies should be adaptable and responsive to ensure relevance and effectiveness.

Measuring Success and Analytics

Social media platforms provide analytics tools that help in measuring the success of marketing campaigns. Realtors can track engagement, reach, and conversion rates to understand the effectiveness of their strategies.

Constant Evolution and Learning

The social media landscape is constantly evolving, with new platforms and features emerging. Staying updated and adapting to these changes is crucial for maintaining an effective social media presence in real estate marketing.

Social media has significantly altered the landscape of real estate marketing. Its ability to build brands, showcase properties, engage with clients, and provide market insights makes it an essential tool for realtors. In the digital age, a well-planned and executed social media strategy can be a game-changer in the competitive world of real estate.

9.5: FUTURE TRENDS IN REAL ESTATE TECHNOLOGY

The landscape of real estate technology is rapidly evolving, promising to introduce new trends and innovations that could reshape the industry. These advancements are expected to make the property buying, selling, and management processes more efficient, accessible, and user-friendly. This section explores the potential future trends in real estate technology and their implications for the market, particularly focusing on how these advancements might manifest in the Maltese real estate sector.

Artificial Intelligence and Machine Learning

Artificial Intelligence (AI) and Machine Learning (ML) are set to play pivotal roles in real estate. AI can analyze large data sets to predict market trends, identify investment opportunities, and provide personalized property recommendations to buyers. ML algorithms can continuously learn from data patterns to enhance predictive analytics in real estate pricing, demand forecasting, and customer preferences.

Blockchain in Real Estate Transactions

Blockchain technology is anticipated to revolutionize real estate transactions by enhancing transparency, security, and efficiency. Smart contracts on blockchain can automate and streamline property transactions, reduce fraud, and provide a transparent record of the property's history.

Internet of Things (IoT) in Property Management

The Internet of Things (IoT) is expected to further integrate into property management, with smart homes becoming increasingly common. IoT devices can help in monitoring and managing property conditions, energy consumption, and security systems, providing convenience and efficiency for homeowners and property managers.

Augmented Reality and Virtual Reality

While VR is already making waves in property viewings, its combination with Augmented Reality (AR) is expected to provide even more immersive experiences. AR can overlay digital information onto physical real estate environments, allowing for interactive property tours and real-time property modifications visualization.

Advanced CRM Systems

Customer Relationship Management (CRM) systems will become more sophisticated, utilizing AI to provide insights into customer behavior and preferences. These systems will aid real estate professionals in tailoring their services to individual clients and improving customer engagement and satisfaction.

Drones for Property Showcasing

Drones will increasingly be used for property showcasing, offering aerial views and virtual tours of properties. This can be particularly beneficial for large estates, commercial properties, or properties with unique geographical features.

Predictive Maintenance in Real Estate

Predictive maintenance, powered by IoT and AI, will become more prevalent. Sensors can predict when a property component might need maintenance, helping to prevent costly repairs and prolong the lifespan of property assets.

Sustainable and Green Technology

Sustainable and green technologies will gain more prominence in real estate. Innovations in energy-efficient construction materials, renewable energy systems, and eco-friendly design principles will play crucial roles in reducing the environmental impact of properties.

5G and Real Estate Operations

The rollout of 5G technology is expected to significantly impact real estate operations, offering faster and more reliable internet connections. This will enhance the capabilities of IoT devices and enable more efficient data processing and real-time analytics.

Proptech Startups and Innovation

The rise of proptech startups is set to introduce innovative solutions to real estate challenges. These startups will drive innovation in various aspects of the industry, from property search platforms to investment analysis tools.

Data Security and Privacy

As technology becomes more integrated into real estate, data security and privacy concerns will become more critical. Advanced cybersecurity measures will be essential to protect sensitive information in real estate transactions and operations.

Virtual Staging and Interior Design

Virtual staging and digital interior design tools will become more sophisticated, allowing sellers and agents to create appealing property interiors digitally. This can help in attracting buyers and renters by showcasing the potential of a space.

Remote and Automated Transactions

The trend towards remote and automated transactions will continue, with technology enabling property transactions to be completed with minimal physical interaction. This includes online document signing, virtual meetings, and digital payments.

Integration of Social Media and Real Estate Platforms

Social media will become more integrated with real estate platforms, offering new avenues for property marketing, customer engagement, and market research.

Customization and Personalization in Property Search

Technology will enable more customization and personalization in property searches. Users will receive property recommendations tailored to their specific preferences and behaviors, improving the property search experience.

Urban Planning and Smart Cities

Technological advancements will play a significant role in urban planning and the development of smart cities. Data analytics and AI will be used to design urban spaces that are efficient, sustainable, and responsive to residents' needs.

Tech-Enabled Real Estate Financing

Technological innovations in real estate financing, such as online mortgage platforms and fintech solutions, will simplify and expedite the financing process for buyers.

The future of real estate technology is bright, with numerous advancements on the horizon that promise to transform the industry. From AI and blockchain to IoT and sustainable technologies, these innovations will streamline processes, enhance user experiences, and open up new possibilities in the real estate sector. As these technologies continue to evolve and become more integrated into the industry, they will offer exciting opportunities for growth, efficiency, and sustainability in the Maltese real estate market and beyond.

CHAPTER 10: RISK MANAGEMENT IN PROPERTY INVESTMENT

Investing in property, while often lucrative, involves various risks that need to be carefully managed. Chapter 10 delves into the vital aspect of risk management in property investment, a crucial consideration for ensuring the longevity and profitability of your real estate ventures. This chapter will explore strategies to identify, assess, and mitigate the inherent risks associated with property investment. From market fluctuations and legal complexities to maintenance issues and tenant management, we'll cover a range of potential challenges and provide practical solutions. Understanding these risks and implementing effective management strategies is essential for any successful property investor, especially in the dynamic Maltese market.

10.1: IDENTIFYING AND MITIGATING RISKS IN REAL ESTATE

Risk management is a crucial aspect of successful real estate investing. It involves identifying potential risks associated with property investment and implementing strategies to mitigate them. Understanding and managing these risks effectively is essential to protect your investment and ensure its profitability, especially in diverse markets like Malta. This section addresses various risks in real estate investment and outlines strategies for mitigating them.

Market Volatility Risk

Real estate markets can be volatile, with prices fluctuating due to economic conditions, interest rates, and market sentiment. To mitigate this risk, conduct thorough market research before investing. Understanding long-term market trends, economic forecasts, and the factors that influence property values in specific areas can help in making informed decisions.

Liquidity Risk

Real estate is not a liquid asset, meaning it cannot be quickly converted to cash without the potential for loss. This risk can be mitigated by maintaining a diversified investment portfolio and having a clear understanding of your long-term financial goals and strategies for property liquidation if necessary.

Credit Risk

If your investment strategy involves lending or borrowing, credit risk becomes a factor. For borrowers, securing a fixed-rate mortgage can mitigate the risk of fluctuating interest rates. For lenders or investors in real estate debt, thoroughly assessing the borrower's creditworthiness is crucial.

Legal and Regulatory Risk

Changes in laws and regulations can impact property investment. To mitigate this risk, stay informed about current and proposed laws related to property ownership, zoning, taxes, and tenant rights. Engaging a legal expert in real estate can provide valuable guidance and help navigate these complexities.

Environmental Risk

Environmental factors such as climate change, natural disasters, and pollution can impact property values and usability. Investing in properties with lower environmental risk profiles and obtaining comprehensive insurance policies can help mitigate these risks.

Tenant and Occupancy Risk

For rental properties, the risk of vacancy and problematic tenants can impact your revenue. Conducting thorough tenant screenings, setting competitive rental prices, and keeping the property well-maintained can help minimize this risk.

Property-Specific Risk

Each property has specific risks based on its condition, location, and type. Conducting a comprehensive property inspection before purchasing can identify potential issues. Investing in regular maintenance and updates can help preserve the property's value and attractiveness to buyers or renters.

Inflation Risk

Inflation can erode the real value of your investment returns. Investing in properties with potential for rental income growth or in areas with appreciating property values can help offset the effects of inflation.

Interest Rate Risk

Fluctuations in interest rates can impact mortgage payments and investment returns. Locking in fixed-rate mortgages can provide stability. For investors, understanding how interest rate changes can affect the real estate market is key to timing your investments.

Diversification Risk

Overconcentration in a single property type or location can increase risk. Diversifying your real estate portfolio across different property types and geographic areas can spread risk and provide more stability.

Technology and Innovation Risk

The rapid pace of technological change can impact real estate markets. Staying informed about technological advancements in construction, property management, and real estate marketing can help you adapt and leverage these changes.

Management and Operational Risk

Effective property management is crucial to mitigate operational risks. This involves managing day-to-day operations efficiently, addressing maintenance issues promptly, and ensuring compliance with legal and regulatory requirements.

Exit Strategy Risk

Not having a clear exit strategy can pose a risk to your investment. Developing a strategic plan for selling or otherwise exiting your investment based on market conditions and your financial goals can help manage this risk.

Insurance and Protection

Obtaining appropriate insurance coverage is a fundamental way to mitigate many real estate risks. This includes property insurance, liability insurance, and, in some cases, additional coverage for specific risks like floods or earthquakes.

Financial Planning and Cash Flow Management

Sound financial planning and effective cash flow management are crucial in real estate investing. Ensure that you have sufficient cash reserves to handle unexpected expenses, vacancies, or market downturns.

Building Relationships with Professionals

Building relationships with real estate professionals, financial advisors, and legal experts can provide you with the support and guidance needed to navigate the complexities of real estate investment and mitigate risks effectively.

Identifying and mitigating risks in real estate requires a comprehensive approach that encompasses market research, financial planning, legal compliance, and effective property management. By understanding the various risks involved and implementing strategies to address them, investors can safeguard their investments and enhance their profitability in the real estate market.

10.2: THE IMPORTANCE OF INSURANCE IN PROPERTY INVESTMENT

Insurance in property investment serves as a critical risk management tool, providing a safeguard against various unforeseen events that could otherwise have devastating financial impacts. Understanding the different types of insurance and their importance is essential for any property investor, particularly in markets like Malta where diverse risks can affect property ownership. This section explores the various insurance policies relevant to property investment and their role in protecting investors from potential losses.

Property Insurance

Property insurance is fundamental for any real estate investment. It provides coverage against damage to the property itself due to events like fire, storms, floods, and other natural disasters. In Malta, where certain areas may be prone to specific environmental risks, ensuring adequate coverage against these is crucial. Property insurance can also cover the cost of repairs or rebuilding in case of significant damage, protecting the investor from substantial financial loss.

Liability Insurance

Liability insurance is crucial for property owners, particularly those renting out their properties. It protects against claims made by third parties for injuries or damage occurring on the property. For instance, if a tenant or visitor is injured due to a fault in the property, liability insurance can cover legal fees and any resulting compensation claims.

Landlord Insurance

For those involved in rental investments, landlord insurance provides coverage beyond standard property insurance. It can include protection against loss of rental income due to property damage, tenant default, and other tenant-related risks. In a dynamic rental market like Malta's, where short-term rentals are common, this type of insurance offers crucial financial protection.

Title Insurance

Title insurance protects against issues related to the property's title, such as disputes over ownership, outstanding liens, or issues with the property's legal description. While title disputes might be less common, having title insurance can provide peace of mind and financial protection in case of legal challenges.

Construction Insurance

For investors involved in property development or significant renovations, construction insurance is important. It covers risks related to the construction process, including material damage, delays, and accidents on site. This insurance is particularly relevant in Malta, given its ongoing development and renovation of historical properties.

Natural Disaster Insurance

In areas prone to specific natural disasters, such as earthquakes or floods, having additional natural disaster insurance can be wise. This type of insurance offers specific coverage for damages caused by these events, which might not be fully covered under standard property insurance policies.

Home Warranty Insurance

Home warranty insurance covers the cost of repairing or replacing major components of a property, like heating systems, plumbing, or electrical wiring. For investors, this insurance can be valuable in managing maintenance costs and ensuring the functionality of essential property systems.

Tenant's Insurance

Encouraging or requiring tenants to have their own renter's insurance can be a prudent strategy. This type of insurance covers tenants' personal property and can provide liability coverage for damages they might cause to the property.

Vacancy Insurance

Properties that remain vacant for extended periods face different risks, such as vandalism or unnoticed damage. Vacancy insurance provides coverage for properties during periods when they are not occupied.

Flood Insurance

In flood-prone areas, standard property insurance policies often do not cover flood damage. Separate flood insurance can provide specific coverage for losses due to flooding, a crucial consideration in certain areas of Malta.

Understanding Policy Details

Understanding the details of insurance policies is essential. This includes knowing the extent of coverage, exclusions, deductibles, and policy limits. Property owners should review their policies regularly and adjust coverage as needed.

Cost vs. Benefit Analysis

Conducting a cost-benefit analysis of different insurance policies is important. While insurance is a necessary expense, choosing the right coverage level involves balancing the cost of premiums against the potential risks and financial impacts.

Insurance as Part of Investment Strategy

Incorporating insurance into the overall investment strategy is key to effective risk management. Insurance should be considered an integral part of the investment's financial planning, ensuring long-term protection and stability.

Insurance for Historical Properties

For investors in historical properties, which are common in Malta, specialized insurance may be required. These properties often have unique risks and may need specific types of coverage due to their age, construction materials, and cultural value.

Consulting with Insurance Professionals

Consulting with insurance professionals who understand real estate investment can provide valuable insights. They can assist in selecting the right policies and ensuring adequate coverage based on the specific risks of the property.

Regular Review and Adjustment

Regularly reviewing and adjusting insurance policies is crucial. As property values change, renovations are made, or new risks emerge, insurance coverage should be updated to reflect these changes.

Insurance plays a vital role in property investment by providing financial protection against a wide range of risks. For investors, having the right insurance coverage is not just a safety net but a strategic component of successful property management and investment. In the ever-evolving real estate market, staying informed and proactive about insurance options can safeguard investments and ensure their long-term viability and profitability.

10.3: ECONOMIC FACTORS AFFECTING REAL ESTATE MARKETS

The real estate market is intricately linked to the broader economy, with various economic factors playing a significant role in shaping market dynamics. Understanding these factors is crucial for investors, as they can significantly impact property values, investment returns, and market opportunities. In this section, we explore the key economic factors affecting real estate markets, particularly focusing on how these elements influence property investments in Malta.

Interest Rates

Interest rates are a primary economic factor influencing the real estate market. Lower interest rates can make borrowing cheaper, stimulating demand for property as mortgages become more affordable. Conversely, higher interest rates can decrease demand, as borrowing costs rise. For investors in Malta, understanding the European Central Bank's interest rate policies is essential, as these rates influence local lending rates.

Economic Growth

Economic growth directly affects real estate markets. A growing economy typically leads to higher employment rates and incomes, which can boost demand for property. In Malta, sectors like tourism, gaming, and financial services significantly contribute to economic growth and, consequently, the real estate market.

Inflation

Inflation impacts the real estate market by affecting property values and rental rates. In an inflationary environment, property prices and rents may increase, as the value of money decreases. Real estate is often considered a hedge against inflation, as property values and rents tend to rise along with inflation.

Government Policies and Incentives

Government policies and incentives can have a significant impact on the real estate market. Tax incentives, subsidies for homebuyers, and development policies can stimulate market growth. In Malta, government initiatives such as the First-Time Buyers Scheme or reduced stamp duties can influence market demand.

Unemployment Rates

The unemployment rate is a critical economic indicator affecting the real estate market. High unemployment can lead to reduced demand for property, as fewer people can afford to buy or rent. Conversely, low unemployment typically boosts market demand.

Consumer Confidence

Consumer confidence reflects the overall sentiment about the economy and can influence real estate market trends. High consumer confidence tends to increase demand for property, as people are more willing to make significant purchases like homes.

Population Growth and Demographics

Population growth and demographic changes significantly impact real estate demand. An increasing population can lead to higher demand for housing. In Malta, factors like immigration, expatriate influx, and an aging population influence housing demand in different segments of the market.

Global Economic Trends

In today's interconnected world, global economic trends can impact local real estate markets. For instance, global financial crises or economic downturns can reduce foreign investment and demand for property.

Real Estate Supply and Development

The supply of real estate and development projects also influences the market. An oversupply of properties can lead to a decrease in prices, while limited supply, especially in desirable areas, can drive prices up. In Malta, development policies and the availability of land for construction play crucial roles in determining market supply.

Foreign Investment

Foreign investment in real estate can significantly affect market dynamics. In Malta, foreign investment, driven by factors like residency programs and a favorable tax regime, influences property demand, particularly in luxury and high-end segments.

Currency Exchange Rates

For markets with significant foreign investment, like Malta, currency exchange rates can influence real estate transactions. Fluctuations in the Euro's value can impact the affordability and attractiveness of properties for foreign investors.

Infrastructure Development

Infrastructure development can enhance property values in its vicinity. In Malta, developments in transportation, utilities, and community amenities can make certain areas more attractive for both residential and commercial properties.

Technology and Innovation

Technological advancements and innovation can impact economic productivity and, subsequently, the real estate market. The growth of sectors like fintech and iGaming in Malta has created new demands for commercial and residential real estate.

Interest of Institutional Investors

The interest of institutional investors in real estate can signal market trends. Their investment patterns in certain types of properties or locations can influence market dynamics and investor confidence.

Real Estate Financing Availability

The availability and terms of real estate financing, including mortgages and investment loans, affect market accessibility. Easier financing conditions can stimulate market activity, while stricter lending criteria can dampen it.

Rental Market Dynamics

The rental market dynamics, including demand and rental yields, are influenced by economic factors. In Malta, rental demand is driven by factors like tourism, expatriate workers, and student populations, impacting investment opportunities in the rental market.

Economic factors play a critical role in shaping the real estate market, influencing property values, investment opportunities, and market trends. For investors in Malta, staying informed about these economic indicators and understanding their implications is key to making informed investment decisions and navigating the market effectively. As these factors are subject to change, continuous monitoring and adaptability are essential for success in the dynamic world of real estate.

10.4: POLITICAL AND REGULATORY CHANGES AND THEIR IMPACT

The real estate market does not operate in isolation; it is significantly influenced by political and regulatory environments. Political stability, government policies, regulatory changes, and legal reforms can all profoundly impact property investment dynamics. This section explores how political and regulatory changes can affect the real estate market, particularly focusing on their implications for property investment in Malta.

Impact of Political Stability on Real Estate

Political stability is a cornerstone of a healthy real estate market. Stable governments and predictable policies encourage investment in property markets. In Malta, political stability has been a key factor in attracting foreign investment in real estate, contributing to the sector's growth and resilience.

Government Policies on Property Ownership

Government policies directly affect the real estate market. Policies regarding property ownership, taxes, and incentives for buyers or developers can either stimulate or dampen market activity. In Malta, policies such as incentives for first-time buyers or tax rebates on property purchases have been instrumental in shaping the market.

Regulatory Changes and Real Estate Investment

Regulatory changes in areas like planning, zoning, and environmental protection can impact real estate investment. Stricter regulations may limit development opportunities, while relaxed regulations can lead to increased development activities. Investors must stay informed about regulatory changes to understand their potential impact on investment opportunities.

Legal Reforms and Property Rights

Legal reforms related to property rights, transaction processes, and dispute resolution can significantly influence real estate investments. Clear and enforceable property rights, along with efficient legal processes, create a favorable environment for real estate transactions.

Taxation Policies and Real Estate

Taxation policies, including property taxes, capital gains taxes, and stamp duties, play a crucial role in real estate investment decisions. Changes in these policies can affect the profitability and attractiveness of property investments. For instance, Malta's favorable tax regime for foreign investors has been a key driver in attracting international property buyers.

Impact of International Politics and Relations

International politics and diplomatic relations can influence the flow of foreign investment in real estate. Policies regarding foreign ownership of property, international sanctions, and bilateral agreements can all affect the attractiveness of a market to international investors.

Housing Policies and Affordable Housing Initiatives

Government initiatives aimed at promoting affordable housing can impact the real estate market, particularly in the residential sector. These policies can affect market demand and supply dynamics, influencing property prices and rental rates.

Environmental Regulations and Sustainable Development

Environmental regulations and policies promoting sustainable development are increasingly influencing real estate development. Stricter environmental standards can increase development costs but also create opportunities for investment in green buildings and sustainable technologies.

Regulatory Response to Market Conditions

Governments often respond to real estate market conditions with regulatory interventions. For example, measures to cool down an overheated housing market or to stimulate a sluggish real estate sector can have immediate and significant impacts.

Urban Planning and Infrastructure Development

Changes in urban planning and infrastructure development policies can greatly affect property values. Investments in transportation, utilities, and public amenities can enhance the attractiveness of certain areas, leading to increased demand for properties in those locations.

Brexit and Its Implications

For countries like Malta with strong ties to the UK, Brexit has had implications in the real estate sector. Changes in the flow of British investment and alterations in residency rights for UK citizens can impact the market.

Rental Market Regulations

Regulations governing the rental market, including tenant rights, rent control, and lease agreements, can affect the attractiveness of investment in rental properties. In Malta, recent changes in rental laws aimed at providing more stability and security for tenants and landlords are an example.

Impact of Election Cycles

Election cycles can bring uncertainty to the real estate market, as impending elections often lead to speculation about potential policy changes. Investors may adopt a 'wait and see' approach during these periods.

Global Economic Policies

Global economic policies, including trade agreements and economic sanctions, can indirectly impact real estate markets. These policies can affect economic growth, foreign investment flows, and currency exchange rates, all of which are relevant to real estate.

Public-Private Partnerships

Public-private partnerships in real estate development can be influenced by political and regulatory changes. Such collaborations for urban development projects or infrastructure improvements can create new investment opportunities.

Technology Regulations in Real Estate

Regulations surrounding emerging technologies in real estate, such as the use of drones for property viewing or blockchain in transactions, can also impact the market. Adoption and regulation of these technologies can open up new avenues for marketing, investing, and managing properties.

Political and regulatory environments play a critical role in shaping the real estate market. For investors in Malta and elsewhere, staying abreast of political developments and regulatory changes is essential to understanding the market landscape and making informed investment decisions. As these factors can have both immediate and long-term impacts, a proactive approach to monitoring and adapting to political and regulatory changes is crucial for successful real estate investment.

10.5: BUILDING A DIVERSE REAL ESTATE PORTFOLIO

Diversification is a fundamental principle in investment, and real estate is no exception. Building a diverse real estate portfolio is crucial for spreading risk and enhancing the potential for returns. This involves investing in different types of properties and locations to balance the portfolio against market fluctuations and economic changes. In this section, we explore the strategies and considerations for building a diverse real estate portfolio, particularly in the context of the dynamic Maltese property market.

Understanding Portfolio Diversification

Diversification in real estate means not putting all your investment eggs in one basket. By spreading investments across different property types (residential, commercial, industrial), geographic locations, and investment strategies (rental income, capital appreciation), investors can reduce risk and increase the likelihood of steady returns.

Mix of Property Types

Investing in a mix of property types is a key strategy for diversification. Residential properties often offer stable rental income, while commercial properties, like office spaces or retail units, can provide higher rental yields but might be more sensitive to economic cycles. Industrial properties or warehouses can offer long-term leases and stability.

Geographical Diversification

Investing in different geographic areas can protect against local market downturns. In the case of Malta, this might mean investing in different regions, each with its unique market dynamics, or considering international investments to spread geographical risk.

Balancing Risk and Returns

Different real estate investments come with varying levels of risk and potential returns. High-growth areas might offer substantial capital appreciation but come with higher risks, while established areas might offer more stability but lower growth potential. A balanced portfolio combines these elements to manage overall risk.

Investment in Emerging Markets

Including properties in emerging markets or growth areas can offer high potential returns. For investors in Malta, this might involve identifying up-and-coming areas or investing in regions undergoing significant development.

Liquidity Considerations

Including some liquid assets in your real estate portfolio, like Real Estate Investment Trusts (REITs), can provide flexibility. REITs offer the advantage of real estate investment without the need for direct property management and with greater liquidity.

Long-term and Short-term Investments

A diverse portfolio includes both long-term and short-term real estate investments. Long-term investments might focus on capital appreciation, while short-term investments might aim to capitalize on quick flips or developments.

Rental Properties for Regular Income

Including rental properties in your portfolio can provide a regular income stream. In Malta, this could include residential rentals, vacation rentals in tourist areas, or commercial properties with long-term leases.

Renovation and Development Projects

Investing in renovation and development projects can offer significant returns but comes with higher risks and the need for more active management. These types of investments can diversify a portfolio that primarily includes more stable, income-generating properties.

Investing in Different Stages of the Property Cycle

Real estate markets move in cycles. Investing in properties at different stages of the cycle can balance out the effects of market ups and downs.

Tax Efficiency and Legal Considerations

Understanding the tax implications and legal considerations of different types of property investments is crucial. This includes considering the tax efficiency of investments and the legal structures used for owning property.

Use of Leverage

Using leverage, or borrowed capital, can enhance returns but also increases risk. A diversified portfolio balances leveraged investments with fully owned properties to manage this risk.

Monitoring and Adjusting the Portfolio

Regularly monitoring the performance of your real estate investments and making adjustments as needed is key to maintaining a healthy, diversified portfolio. This includes staying informed about market changes, economic trends, and adjusting your strategy accordingly.

Professional Advice and Management

Seeking professional advice from real estate experts, financial advisors, and legal professionals can aid in building a diversified portfolio. These professionals can provide insights into market trends, investment opportunities, and risk management strategies.

Sustainable and Eco-Friendly Investments

Incorporating sustainable and eco-friendly properties can add a new dimension to your portfolio. These properties are increasingly in demand and can offer long-term cost savings and environmental benefits.

Technology and Real Estate Investments

Utilizing technology for real estate investments, such as property management software or investment platforms, can provide insights and efficiency in managing a diverse portfolio.

Educational Investments and Continuous Learning

Continuous learning and staying educated about real estate trends, investment strategies, and market dynamics are essential for successfully diversifying and managing a real estate portfolio.

Building a diverse real estate portfolio requires a strategic approach that balances different types of properties, investment strategies, and geographic locations. By carefully selecting investments that complement each other and spreading risk across different market segments, investors can create a robust and resilient property portfolio. This approach not only reduces exposure to market volatility but also positions the investor to capitalize on a wide range of opportunities, ensuring long-term growth and stability in their real estate endeavors.

CHAPTER 11:
POST-PURCHASE CONSIDERATIONS

The journey of real estate investment doesn't end with the purchase of a property. Post-purchase considerations play a crucial role in maximizing the return on investment and ensuring the smooth management of the property. Chapter 11 delves into the essential aspects that property investors must address after acquiring real estate. From effective property management and maintenance strategies to dealing with legalities, taxes, and tenant relations, this chapter provides a comprehensive guide to the post-purchase landscape. It's designed to equip investors, especially in diverse markets like Malta, with the knowledge and tools necessary for successful long-term property management and investment growth.

11.1: PROPERTY MANAGEMENT ESSENTIALS

Effective property management is a critical component of successful real estate investment. It encompasses a broad range of responsibilities, from maintaining the property to managing tenant relations, all aimed at maximizing the property's value and profitability. This section outlines the essential elements of property management, offering insights and strategies for managing real estate investments efficiently and effectively.

Regular Property Maintenance

Maintaining the property in top condition is essential to preserve its value and appeal. Regular maintenance includes routine inspections, timely repairs, and upkeep of common areas. Preventative maintenance, such as servicing HVAC systems or inspecting roofs, can help avoid costly major repairs in the future.

Financial Management and Record-Keeping

Effective financial management is crucial in property management. This involves collecting rent, managing expenses, and maintaining accurate records for accounting and tax purposes. Utilizing property management software can streamline these tasks, ensuring efficient tracking and management of financial transactions.

Tenant Screening and Relationship Management

Finding and retaining reliable tenants is a key aspect of property management. Thorough tenant screening, including credit checks, references, and background checks, can help secure responsible occupants. Building positive relationships with tenants through good communication and prompt response to concerns can lead to higher tenant satisfaction and retention.

Understanding Legal Obligations

Property managers must be well-versed in the legal aspects of property rental and ownership. This includes understanding lease agreements, adhering to local housing laws and regulations, and ensuring compliance with safety and health standards.

Effective Marketing and Leasing Strategies

Marketing the property effectively to attract tenants is another crucial aspect. This includes advertising the property through various channels, conducting viewings, and negotiating lease terms. A well-crafted leasing strategy can minimize vacancy periods and ensure a steady income stream.

Dealing with Repairs and Emergencies

Prompt and efficient handling of repairs and emergencies is vital in property management. Having a network of reliable contractors and service providers can ensure that issues are addressed quickly, minimizing inconvenience to tenants and potential damage to the property.

Implementing Sustainable Practices

Incorporating sustainable practices in property management, such as energy-efficient systems and eco-friendly maintenance practices, can reduce operating costs and appeal to environmentally conscious tenants.

Maximizing Rental Income

Strategically setting and adjusting rental prices based on market conditions is important to maximize income while maintaining competitiveness. Regular market analysis can inform appropriate rental pricing strategies.

Handling Tenant Disputes and Evictions

Managing tenant disputes professionally and legally is an important skill for property managers. Understanding the eviction process and handling it in compliance with legal requirements is essential in cases where disputes cannot be resolved amicably.

Utilizing Technology in Property Management

Leveraging technology in property management, such as online rent payment systems, digital lease agreements, and property management apps, can enhance efficiency and convenience for both managers and tenants.

Risk Management

Identifying and mitigating risks associated with property ownership, such as liability risks or potential property damage, is a key responsibility. This includes ensuring adequate insurance coverage and implementing safety measures.

Periodic Property Evaluations

Conducting periodic evaluations of the property can help in assessing its condition, identifying needs for upgrades or renovations, and evaluating its market value.

Tenant Retention Strategies

Implementing tenant retention strategies, such as regular communication, addressing concerns promptly, and providing incentives for lease renewals, can reduce turnover and associated costs.

Property Upgrades and Renovations

Considering property upgrades and renovations can enhance the property's appeal and value. These should be carefully planned to ensure they are cost-effective and aligned with market demands.

Engaging with Local Communities

Engaging with the local community can enhance the property's reputation and desirability. This might include participating in local events, supporting community projects, or maintaining good relationships with neighborhood entities.

Managing Multiple Properties

For investors with multiple properties, efficient management involves coordination and scalability. This might require a team approach or the engagement of professional property management firms.

Preparing for Property Sale

If selling the property is part of the investment strategy, preparing for the sale is a key aspect of management. This includes maintaining the property in excellent condition, keeping detailed records, and understanding market timing.

Effective property management is a multifaceted endeavor that requires diligence, organization, and a proactive approach. By focusing on these essential elements, property investors can ensure their real estate assets are well-maintained, financially viable, and attractive to tenants, ultimately leading to sustained investment success.

11.2: UNDERSTANDING MAINTENANCE AND UPKEEP RESPONSIBILITIES

Maintenance and upkeep are crucial aspects of property ownership, directly impacting the property's value, safety, and appeal to tenants or buyers. Effective maintenance not only prevents minor issues from becoming major problems but also ensures that the property remains a desirable and competitive asset in the market. This section focuses on the key responsibilities involved in property maintenance and upkeep, highlighting best practices for ensuring properties are well-cared for and retain their value over time.

Regular Inspections and Preventative Maintenance

Conducting regular inspections is fundamental to proactive property maintenance. These inspections help identify potential issues before they escalate into major problems. Preventative maintenance tasks, such as servicing heating systems, checking for leaks, and ensuring electrical systems are up to code, are essential for avoiding costly repairs in the future.

Responding to Repairs Promptly

A swift response to repair needs is critical in property management. Addressing repair issues promptly not only prevents further damage but also shows tenants that their comfort and safety are priorities. This can lead to higher tenant satisfaction and retention rates.

Budgeting for Maintenance and Repairs

Allocating a budget for maintenance and repairs is essential. It's recommended to set aside a certain percentage of the rental income or property value annually for maintenance needs. This financial planning helps in managing expenses effectively and ensures that funds are available when needed.

Landscaping and Exterior Maintenance

Maintaining the property's exterior and landscaping is important for curb appeal and can significantly impact a property's perceived value. Regular tasks include lawn care, garden maintenance, exterior painting, and ensuring walkways and driveways are in good condition.

Safety and Compliance with Regulations

Ensuring the property complies with safety and building regulations is a legal responsibility of property owners. This includes installing and maintaining smoke detectors, ensuring adequate fire exits, and adhering to health and safety standards.

Energy Efficiency and Sustainability

Investing in energy efficiency upgrades can reduce utility costs and appeal to environmentally conscious tenants. This can include installing energy-efficient appliances, upgrading insulation, or implementing renewable energy sources like solar panels.

Tenant Responsibilities and Education

Clearly communicating maintenance responsibilities to tenants is important. Educating tenants on their responsibilities, such as changing light bulbs or reporting maintenance issues, can help in maintaining the property effectively.

Working with Reliable Contractors

Building relationships with reliable contractors and service providers ensures that maintenance and repair work is carried out efficiently and to a high standard. Having a network of trusted professionals can also expedite the repair process.

Modernization and Upgrades

Periodically upgrading and modernizing the property can enhance its value and appeal. This could involve updating kitchen appliances, bathroom fixtures, or implementing smart home technology.

Record-Keeping and Documentation

Maintaining detailed records of all maintenance and repair work is essential. This documentation can be valuable for insurance claims, tax purposes, and future property evaluations.

Seasonal Maintenance

Implementing seasonal maintenance routines can protect the property from weather-related damage. This includes tasks like cleaning gutters, checking heating systems before winter, and ensuring proper ventilation during summer.

Handling Emergency Repairs

Having a plan for emergency repairs is crucial. This includes having contact information for emergency service providers and a process for tenants to report emergencies.

Pest Control and Prevention

Regular pest control is essential to maintain a healthy living environment. Preventative measures and prompt treatment of infestations are important to keep the property pest-free.

Handling Wear and Tear

Understanding the difference between normal wear and tear versus damage caused by tenants is important for property upkeep and security deposit assessments.

Interior Maintenance

Regular interior maintenance, such as painting, fixing fixtures, and repairing flooring, keeps the property looking fresh and well-maintained.

Investing in Long-Term Solutions

Opting for long-term maintenance solutions rather than quick fixes can be more cost-effective in the long run. This includes choosing quality materials and sustainable practices.

Community Rules and Standards

For properties in communities with homeowners' associations or similar entities, adhering to community maintenance rules and standards is essential.

Maintenance and upkeep responsibilities are integral to preserving and enhancing the value of a property. By implementing a systematic approach to regular maintenance, addressing repairs promptly, and planning for long-term property care, investors can ensure their real estate assets remain attractive and valuable in the competitive market. This proactive approach to property maintenance not only protects the investment but also contributes to the satisfaction and safety of tenants or residents, reinforcing the property's reputation and desirability.

11.3: ENGAGING WITH THE COMMUNITY AND NEIGHBORS

Engaging with the community and neighbors is a pivotal aspect of property ownership and management that often gets overlooked. However, fostering good relationships with the community can lead to a more harmonious living environment and can even positively impact the value and appeal of a property. This section explores the importance of community engagement and strategies to effectively interact and build relationships with neighbors and the local community, especially in diverse and closely-knit societies like Malta.

Understanding the Local Community

The first step in engaging with the community is understanding its dynamics. This involves getting to know the area's history, culture, demographics, and key issues. In Malta, with its rich history and strong community ties, understanding local traditions and customs is essential for building rapport with neighbors.

Participating in Local Events and Activities

Active participation in local events, festivals, and community activities is a great way to integrate into the community. Involvement in such activities demonstrates a commitment to the local culture and helps in building relationships with neighbors.

Effective Communication with Neighbors

Open and honest communication is the foundation of good neighborly relations. Introduce yourself to your neighbors and be approachable. Regular, friendly interactions can foster a sense of community and mutual respect.

Respecting Local Norms and Practices

Adhering to local norms and practices is crucial in maintaining harmonious relations. This includes respecting noise levels, property boundaries, and community rules. In Malta, where community living is prevalent, being mindful of local practices and festivals is important.

Contributing to Community Projects

Contributing to community projects or local charities can positively impact the neighborhood. This could include sponsoring local events, participating in community improvement projects, or supporting local causes.

Addressing Community Concerns

Being responsive to community concerns, especially those that directly or indirectly involve your property, is important. Whether it's addressing noise complaints, parking issues, or property maintenance, responsiveness shows that you value your neighbors' comfort and wellbeing.

Creating a Neighborhood Network

Creating or participating in a neighborhood network, such as a residents' association or community group, can facilitate better communication and cooperation among neighbors. This can be especially useful for addressing common concerns or organizing community events.

Encouraging Tenant Involvement

If you're renting out the property, encourage your tenants to be involved in the community. Tenants who feel connected to their community are more likely to take care of the property and maintain good relationships with neighbors.

Promoting Safety and Security

Collaborating with neighbors on safety and security measures can benefit the entire community. This might include neighborhood watch programs or shared security initiatives.

Resolving Disputes Amicably

In case of disputes with neighbors, aim to resolve issues amicably. Open dialogue and compromise can often resolve conflicts without the need for external intervention.

Supporting Local Businesses

Supporting local businesses and services not only contributes to the local economy but also helps in building connections within the community. Patronizing local shops, restaurants, and services is a simple way to integrate and show support for the community.

Engaging in Environmental Conservation

Participating in or initiating environmental conservation efforts, such as clean-up drives or tree planting, can enhance the community's quality of life and environment.

Being a Responsible Property Owner

Being a responsible property owner, by maintaining your property and adhering to local regulations, sets a positive example and contributes to the overall well-being of the community.

Hosting Community Events

Hosting or organizing community events, such as neighborhood gatherings or open houses, can be an effective way to strengthen community bonds and foster a friendly environment.

Utilizing Social Media and Online Platforms

Social media and online platforms can be used to engage with the community, share information, and stay updated on local news and events.

Cultural Sensitivity and Inclusion

In culturally diverse communities, being sensitive and inclusive of different cultural practices and traditions is key to harmonious living.

Feedback and Collaboration

Seeking feedback from neighbors and collaborating on shared concerns can lead to better understanding and solutions that benefit the entire community.

Engaging with the community and neighbors is an integral part of property ownership and management. It not only fosters a positive living environment but also contributes to the property's and the neighborhood's overall appeal and value. Building strong community ties requires effort, understanding, and respect, but the rewards in terms of a supportive and harmonious environment are well worth it, particularly in places like Malta, where community is at the heart of everyday life.

11.4: DEALING WITH TENANTS AND RENTAL AGREEMENTS

Effective management of tenant relationships and rental agreements is a fundamental aspect of successful property investment. This task involves not only finding and retaining reliable tenants but also understanding and adhering to legal requirements related to rental agreements. In this comprehensive exploration, we delve into the best practices for managing tenant relations and the intricacies of rental agreements, with a focus on ensuring a harmonious landlord-tenant relationship and safeguarding the property owner's interests.

Finding the Right Tenants

The process of finding the right tenants is crucial. This involves advertising the property effectively, conducting thorough tenant screenings, and verifying references. The screening process should assess the tenant's ability to pay rent, their rental history, and overall reliability.

Creating Comprehensive Rental Agreements

A comprehensive rental agreement is the foundation of a good landlord-tenant relationship. The agreement should clearly outline the terms and conditions of the rental, including rent amount, payment due dates, security deposit details, maintenance responsibilities, and any house rules.

Understanding Legal Obligations

Landlords must be well-versed in the legal obligations regarding rental properties. This includes adhering to housing laws, respecting tenant rights, and ensuring the property meets safety and health standards. In Malta, being familiar with local tenancy laws is essential to ensure compliance.

Effective Communication

Effective communication is key to maintaining a positive relationship with tenants. Be clear, respectful, and responsive to tenant queries and concerns. Establishing open lines of communication can prevent misunderstandings and resolve issues promptly.

Regular Property Inspections

Conducting regular property inspections helps in maintaining the property's condition and addressing any maintenance issues. These inspections should be carried out respectfully and with prior notice to the tenant.

Handling Maintenance and Repairs

Timely handling of maintenance and repair requests is important for tenant satisfaction and property upkeep. Landlords should either address repair issues promptly themselves or engage reliable contractors to carry out the necessary work.

Rent Collection and Increases

Establishing a systematic rent collection process is crucial. Consider using digital payment methods for convenience. Any rent increases should be done in accordance with the rental agreement and legal requirements, and with adequate notice to the tenant.

Dealing with Late Payments and Evictions

Have clear policies in place for dealing with late payments. In cases where eviction becomes necessary, ensure that it is carried out legally and respectfully, following the proper legal procedures.

Renewals and End of Tenancy

Manage lease renewals efficiently, taking into consideration market conditions and tenant performance. At the end of a tenancy, conduct a thorough inspection, manage the return of the security deposit appropriately, and prepare the property for the next tenant.

Tenant Retention Strategies

Implementing tenant retention strategies, such as timely property upgrades, responsive maintenance, and occasional incentives can lead to longer tenancy periods, reducing vacancy rates and turnover costs.

Updating Rental Agreements

Regularly review and update rental agreements to reflect any changes in laws, market conditions, or property policies. Keeping rental agreements current can help avoid legal issues and ensure they remain relevant and fair.

Documenting Everything

Maintain detailed documentation of all interactions, agreements, inspections, and transactions with tenants. Good record-keeping can be invaluable in case of disputes or legal issues.

Respecting Privacy and Boundaries

Respecting tenant privacy and adhering to boundaries is essential. Always provide notice before visiting the property and avoid unnecessary intrusions into the tenant's space.

Dispute Resolution

Have a plan in place for dispute resolution. Attempt to resolve conflicts amicably through discussion and negotiation before resorting to legal action.

Insurance for Rental Properties

Ensure adequate insurance coverage for rental properties, including liability and loss of rental income coverage. This protects the landlord from potential financial losses related to tenant-related issues.

Cultural Sensitivity and Inclusivity

In diverse communities, being culturally sensitive and inclusive is important for maintaining a harmonious tenant-landlord relationship. This includes understanding and respecting tenants' cultural backgrounds and practices.

Utilizing Property Management Services

For landlords who prefer not to manage tenant relationships directly, professional property management services can be an effective solution. These services handle all aspects of tenant management, from screening to maintenance requests.

Managing tenant relationships and rental agreements effectively is essential for the success of a rental property investment. By focusing on clear communication, legal compliance, and respectful dealings with tenants, landlords can create a positive and productive rental experience. This approach not only ensures tenant satisfaction but also contributes to the long-term value and profitability of the property.

11.5: LONG-TERM STRATEGIC PLANNING FOR PROPERTY OWNERS

Long-term strategic planning is essential for property owners to ensure the sustained growth, profitability, and value of their real estate investments. This approach involves setting long-term goals, anticipating future market trends, and making informed decisions that align with both current and future property market scenarios. In this section, we discuss the key components of long-term strategic planning for property owners, focusing on methods to optimize the value and performance of real estate assets over time.

Setting Long-term Investment Goals

The foundation of strategic planning is setting clear, realistic long-term investment goals. These goals could range from generating steady rental income to achieving significant capital appreciation. Understanding your investment objectives helps in making decisions aligned with your long-term financial and personal aspirations.

Market Research and Analysis

Continuous market research and analysis are crucial for long-term planning. This involves staying informed about local and global real estate market trends, economic factors, demographic shifts, and emerging property technologies. For property owners in Malta, this means keeping a close eye on both domestic market dynamics and international factors that could influence the local market.

Diversification of Property Portfolio

Diversification is a key strategy in long-term planning. By investing in different types of properties and markets, you can spread risk and increase the chances of stable returns. Diversification can involve investing in different property sectors, geographic locations, or even different types of real estate investment vehicles.

Regular Property Reviews and Assessments

Conducting regular reviews and assessments of your property helps in identifying areas that require maintenance, upgrades, or renovations. This proactive approach ensures that your property remains competitive and appealing in the market.

Financial Planning and Cash Flow Management

Effective financial planning and cash flow management are integral to long-term property investment. This includes creating a budget for expenses, setting aside funds for maintenance and emergencies, and planning for potential changes in the market that could affect rental income or property values.

Risk Assessment and Mitigation

Identifying potential risks and developing strategies to mitigate them is crucial for long-term success. This could involve having contingency plans for market downturns, changing tenant demographics, or regulatory changes.

Sustainable and Eco-friendly Investments

Incorporating sustainable and eco-friendly features in properties can not only reduce long-term operational costs but also increase the appeal of the property to environmentally conscious tenants or buyers.

Adapting to Technological Advancements

Staying abreast of technological advancements in the real estate sector and incorporating relevant technologies can enhance property management efficiency and tenant satisfaction. This includes adopting property management software, smart home technologies, and online marketing tools.

Building Strong Tenant Relationships

Establishing and maintaining strong relationships with tenants can lead to higher retention rates, reducing vacancy periods and turnover costs. Good tenant relationships are built on effective communication, responsiveness to tenant needs, and fair and respectful treatment.

Planning for Property Succession

Long-term planning should also include considerations for property succession. This involves making arrangements for the future ownership and management of your properties, ensuring a smooth transition and the continued success of your investments.

Engaging with Professional Advisors

Collaborating with professional advisors such as real estate agents, financial planners, and legal experts can provide valuable insights and guidance in your long-term strategic planning.

Leveraging Financing Options

Understanding and leveraging various financing options can aid in expanding your portfolio or investing in property upgrades. This includes mortgages, refinancing options, and leveraging equity in existing properties.

Investment in Property Upgrades

Investing in periodic upgrades and modernizations can significantly enhance the value and marketability of your property. Keeping properties updated with current trends and amenities can attract higher-quality tenants and justify higher rental rates.

Exit Strategies

Having clear exit strategies for your properties is an important aspect of long-term planning. This might involve selling properties at strategic times or restructuring your portfolio to align with changing market conditions and investment goals.

Community Engagement and Local Regulations

Staying engaged with the local community and staying updated on local regulations and zoning laws can provide insights into potential opportunities or challenges that could affect your properties.

Monitoring Real Estate Legal Changes

Keeping track of legal changes in real estate, such as landlord-tenant laws, tax laws, and building codes, ensures that your investment practices remain compliant and efficient.

Strategic long-term planning is vital for property owners to navigate the complexities of the real estate market successfully. By setting clear goals, staying informed about market trends, managing financial aspects prudently, and being adaptable to changes, property owners can optimize their investments and achieve sustained growth and profitability in their real estate endeavors.

CHAPTER 12:
FUTURE PROSPECTS IN MALTESE REAL ESTATE

As we look towards the future, the Maltese real estate market presents a landscape brimming with both opportunities and challenges. Chapter 12 delves into the potential future prospects of real estate in Malta, exploring emerging trends, market predictions, and the evolving dynamics of this vibrant sector. This chapter aims to equip investors, homeowners, and industry professionals with insights into the factors shaping the future of Maltese real estate. From demographic shifts and economic policies to technological advancements and environmental considerations, we will analyze how these elements are poised to influence the market, offering a comprehensive outlook on the potential trajectories of property investment in Malta.

12.1: PREDICTING MARKET TRENDS AND THEIR IMPACT

Predicting market trends in real estate is vital for making informed investment decisions. Understanding these trends helps investors to anticipate changes, capitalize on opportunities, and mitigate risks. In the context of the Maltese real estate market, various factors contribute to shaping these trends. This section explores the key drivers of market trends in Malta and their potential impact on the real estate landscape.

Economic Growth and Real Estate Demand

Economic growth is a primary driver of real estate demand. In Malta, sectors like tourism, technology, and financial services significantly contribute to the economy. Growth in these sectors can lead to increased demand for both residential and commercial properties. Investors should monitor economic indicators and sector-specific growth to predict changes in real estate demand.

Population Dynamics

Changes in population size, age distribution, and demographics greatly influence real estate trends. In Malta, factors such as an aging population, immigration, and expatriate influx affect housing demands. Understanding these dynamics can provide insights into what types of properties will be in demand in the future.

Urbanization and Development Policies

Urbanization trends and government development policies also shape market dynamics. In Malta, the concentration of development in specific regions and the government's stance on urban development can impact property values and investment opportunities.

Interest Rates and Financing Availability

Interest rates and the availability of financing are crucial factors in real estate market trends. Lower interest rates typically stimulate market activity by making borrowing more affordable, while higher rates can dampen it. Monitoring monetary policies and mortgage market trends in Malta can provide indications of future market directions.

Technology in Real Estate

Advancements in technology, such as virtual property tours, online real estate platforms, and smart home features, are changing how properties are marketed, sold, and managed. Adopting and adapting to these technological trends can be a critical factor in the success of real estate investments.

Environmental Sustainability and Green Buildings

Increasing focus on environmental sustainability and green buildings is influencing buyer preferences and market trends. Properties that incorporate sustainable features or are located in environmentally conscious communities may see increased demand.

Global Economic and Political Factors

The Maltese real estate market, like many others, is influenced by global economic and political events. Issues such as global financial crises, geopolitical tensions, or changes in foreign investment policies can have ripple effects on the local market.

Rental Market Trends

Changes in the rental market, influenced by factors like tourism trends, expatriate population, and local housing policies, can impact investment strategies. Tracking these trends can help predict future rental demand and yield potentials.

Impact of Infrastructure Development

Infrastructure developments, such as new transportation links, community facilities, or technology hubs, can significantly impact property values in surrounding areas. Keeping track of ongoing and planned infrastructure projects in Malta is crucial for anticipating market shifts.

Property Supply and Construction Trends

The balance between property supply and demand is a key market indicator. In Malta, construction trends, regulatory changes in building permissions, and the pace of new developments can influence market supply and, consequently, property prices.

Changing Consumer Preferences

Consumer preferences, driven by lifestyle changes, cultural shifts, or generational differences, can shape real estate trends. For instance, increased demand for flexible living spaces or home offices can create new investment niches.

Impact of Tourism on Real Estate

In Malta, tourism significantly impacts the real estate market, particularly in terms of short-term rentals and holiday homes. Trends in the tourism industry can provide valuable insights into potential investment opportunities.

Investment in Heritage and Cultural Properties

Interest in heritage and cultural properties, especially in a historically rich country like Malta, can influence market trends. These properties often attract a niche market and can offer unique investment opportunities.

Real Estate as a Safe Haven Investment

In times of economic uncertainty, real estate is often seen as a safe haven investment. Monitoring broader economic trends can help predict influxes into the real estate market during such periods.

Regulatory Changes and Legal Framework

Changes in the regulatory and legal framework governing real estate can have significant impacts. Keeping abreast of legislative changes in Malta, such as those related to property taxes, rental laws, or foreign ownership, is essential.

Predicting market trends in real estate requires a multifaceted approach, considering economic, demographic, technological, and regulatory factors. For investors in the Maltese real estate market, staying informed and adaptable to these changing trends is key to identifying opportunities and mitigating risks. Understanding these market drivers enables investors to make strategic decisions that align with the anticipated direction of the market, positioning them for success in a dynamic and evolving real estate landscape.

12.2: OPPORTUNITIES IN COMMERCIAL VS. RESIDENTIAL REAL ESTATE

Investing in real estate offers a spectrum of opportunities across commercial and residential sectors, each with its unique attributes and potential returns. Understanding the differences and opportunities in these sectors is crucial for investors, particularly in Malta's dynamic property market. This section examines the characteristics, risks, and potential rewards of investing in both commercial and residential real estate, providing insights into how investors can navigate these sectors effectively.

Commercial Real Estate Opportunities

1. **Diverse Property Types**: Commercial real estate in Malta encompasses various types, including office spaces, retail units, warehouses, and hospitality venues. Each type offers different investment dynamics and opportunities.

2. **Long-term Leases**: Commercial properties often come with longer lease terms compared to residential properties. This can provide investors with more stable and predictable income streams.

3. **Higher Rental Yields**: Commercial properties generally offer higher rental yields than residential properties. The return on investment can be substantial, though it often comes with higher upfront costs and maintenance expenses.

4. **Economic Sensitivity**: The performance of commercial real estate is closely tied to the economic climate. A booming economy can lead to increased demand for commercial spaces, while an economic downturn can have the opposite effect.

5. **Professional Tenant Relationships**: Tenants of commercial properties are usually businesses, leading to more professional and formal landlord-tenant

relationships. This can simplify management but requires an understanding of commercial leases and business needs.

6. **Impact of Development and Infrastructure**: The value of commercial real estate is often influenced by infrastructure developments, business growth in the area, and urban planning policies.

Residential Real Estate Opportunities

1. **Consistent Demand**: There is a consistent demand for residential properties, driven by fundamental needs for housing. This can provide a level of market stability.

2. **Shorter Lease Terms**: Residential properties typically have shorter lease terms, offering flexibility to adjust rents and terms more frequently. This can be advantageous in a rapidly changing market.

3. **Lower Entry Barriers**: Investing in residential real estate often requires a lower initial investment compared to commercial properties. This makes it accessible to a broader range of investors.

4. **Emotional Appeal**: Residential properties can have an emotional appeal to buyers and renters, which can be leveraged in marketing and tenant retention strategies.

5. **Diverse Investment Options**: The residential sector offers a variety of investment options, from single-family homes to apartments and vacation rentals.

6. **Impact of Local Amenities and Lifestyle Factors**: The value and appeal of residential properties are greatly influenced by local amenities, schools, community facilities, and lifestyle factors.

Comparative Risks and Considerations

1. **Market Fluctuations**: Both sectors are subject to market fluctuations, but they may react differently to economic

changes. Diversification across both types can mitigate overall portfolio risk.

2. **Management Intensity**: Residential properties typically require more hands-on management than commercial properties, especially in the case of short-term rentals or vacation properties.

3. **Regulatory Environment**: The regulatory environment for residential properties, especially regarding tenant rights and rental agreements, can be more stringent than for commercial properties.

4. **Financing and Liquidity**: Financing requirements and liquidity differ between commercial and residential properties. Commercial real estate often requires more substantial capital and may be less liquid.

5. **Economic and Social Trends**: Understanding both economic and social trends is crucial. For instance, the rise in remote working can influence both residential and commercial property demands.

6. **Sustainability and Environmental Considerations**: Investors are increasingly considering sustainability and environmental impact in their investment decisions. This trend is evident in both commercial and residential sectors, with a growing preference for eco-friendly properties.

Both commercial and residential real estate offer distinct opportunities and challenges. For investors in Malta, considering factors such as market trends, economic climate, property types, and management requirements is key to making informed investment decisions. Balancing investments between these two sectors can provide diversification benefits, helping to stabilize returns and reduce overall portfolio risk. By understanding the unique dynamics of each sector, investors can strategically position themselves to capitalize on the diverse opportunities presented in the Maltese real estate market.

12.3: THE ROLE OF GOVERNMENT POLICIES IN SHAPING THE MARKET

Government policies play a pivotal role in shaping the real estate market. These policies can influence market dynamics, affect property prices, and determine investment attractiveness. In Malta, a country with a robust and evolving real estate sector, understanding the impact of government policies is crucial for investors and property owners. This section explores how various government interventions and policies can shape the real estate market in Malta.

Regulatory Frameworks and Real Estate Development

1. **Zoning Laws and Building Regulations**: Zoning laws and building regulations directly impact real estate development. In Malta, these regulations determine what can be built, where, and how, influencing the supply and type of properties available.

2. **Urban Development Policies**: Urban development policies, including plans for infrastructure and public amenities, can significantly affect property values. Well-planned areas with good infrastructure tend to attract more investment and command higher property prices.

3. **Historical Preservation Regulations**: Malta's rich historical heritage means that preservation regulations are crucial. These regulations can impact property prices and development potential, particularly in culturally significant areas.

Taxation and Real Estate Investment

1. **Property Taxes**: The structure of property taxes, including stamp duties and capital gains tax, influences investment decisions. Changes in these tax policies can make real estate investment more or less attractive.

2. **Incentives for Buyers and Developers**: Tax incentives for first-time buyers, subsidies for development projects, and rebates for specific categories of investors can stimulate the real estate market.

3. **VAT and Real Estate Transactions**: The application of VAT to real estate transactions affects the overall cost of buying or developing properties, influencing market activity.

Government Initiatives and Programs

1. **Affordable Housing Schemes**: Government initiatives aimed at promoting affordable housing can impact market dynamics, especially in the residential sector. These schemes can affect demand and supply, influencing property prices and rental rates.

2. **Foreign Investment Policies**: Policies regarding foreign ownership of property, residency programs, and investment schemes can attract or deter foreign investment in the real estate market.

3. **Sustainability and Green Building Initiatives**: Government policies promoting sustainable development and green building practices can drive market trends towards more environmentally friendly properties.

Economic Policies and Market Stability

1. **Monetary and Fiscal Policies**: The government's monetary and fiscal policies, including interest rates and public spending, have indirect but significant impacts on the real estate market.

2. **Economic Stability and Confidence**: The overall economic stability and investor confidence, influenced by government policies, can affect real estate market trends.

Housing Market Interventions

1. **Rent Control and Tenant Protection Laws**: Policies related to rent control and tenant rights can influence the rental market's attractiveness for investors.

2. **Social Housing Programs**: Social housing programs and government-funded housing projects can impact the supply and demand dynamics in the housing market.

Government-Sponsored Development Projects

1. **Public-Private Partnerships**: Public-private partnerships in real estate development can open up new investment opportunities and shape market trends.

2. **Infrastructure Projects**: Large-scale infrastructure projects, like transportation networks and utility upgrades, can significantly enhance property values in surrounding areas.

Impact of Global and EU Policies

1. **EU Regulations and Directives**: As an EU member state, Malta's real estate market is also influenced by EU regulations and directives, impacting everything from environmental standards to investment policies.

2. **International Trade Agreements**: International trade agreements can affect economic growth and foreign investment, indirectly impacting the real estate market.

Crisis Management and Real Estate

1. **Government Response to Economic Crises**: The government's response to economic crises, such as financial bailouts or stimulus packages, can stabilize or revive the real estate market during downturns.

2. **Emergency Measures**: Emergency measures, like moratoriums on evictions during crises, can temporarily impact the rental market.

Government policies are instrumental in shaping the real estate market in Malta. They influence investment trends, property prices, market stability, and the overall attractiveness of the real estate sector. For investors and property owners, staying informed about current and prospective government policies is essential for making strategic decisions and navigating the market effectively. Understanding the interplay between government interventions and market dynamics enables stakeholders to anticipate changes, seize opportunities, and mitigate risks in the evolving landscape of Malta's real estate sector.

12.4: INTERNATIONAL PERSPECTIVES ON MALTESE REAL ESTATE

Maltese real estate has increasingly become a focal point for international investors, owing to its unique characteristics and strategic Mediterranean location. This global interest brings a range of perspectives and influences to the Maltese property market. In this section, we delve into how international factors impact Maltese real estate, examining the nuances that global investors bring to the market and how international trends shape the local real estate landscape.

Attractiveness to Foreign Investors

1. **Strategic Location**: Malta's strategic position in the Mediterranean makes it attractive for international investors looking for a gateway to European and North African markets. This geographical advantage boosts demand, particularly in the commercial real estate sector.

2. **Stable Economy and EU Membership**: Malta's stable economy and its status as an EU member state make it a safe and attractive destination for international property investors. EU membership offers legal and economic stability, which is a significant draw for foreign investors.

3. **Tourism and Hospitality Market**: Malta's robust tourism sector contributes to the appeal of investing in vacation properties, resorts, and hospitality-related real estate. The island's rich history, culture, and natural beauty make it a popular tourist destination, impacting short-term rental markets and hotel developments.

Impact of Foreign Direct Investment (FDI)

1. **Economic Growth and Real Estate Demand**: FDI contributes significantly to Malta's economic growth, with a positive spill-over effect on the real estate market. Increased economic activities create demand for

commercial spaces, residential properties for expatriates, and industrial real estate.

2. **Luxury and High-end Property Segment**: FDI has led to the development of the luxury and high-end property segment in Malta. This includes upscale residential developments, high-rise towers, and exclusive properties catering to affluent international buyers.

Influence of Global Real Estate Trends

1. **Sustainable and Eco-friendly Developments**: Global trends towards sustainability and eco-friendliness influence Maltese real estate developments. International investors are increasingly interested in properties that adhere to green building standards and sustainable practices.

2. **Technological Advancements in Real Estate**: Global technological advancements, like smart home technology and online real estate platforms, are being adopted in the Maltese market, transforming how properties are marketed, sold, and managed.

Regulatory Environment and International Compliance

1. **Anti-Money Laundering (AML) Regulations**: Malta, like other jurisdictions, adheres to international AML regulations. This impacts the real estate sector, with stringent checks and compliance measures for property transactions, particularly involving foreign investors.

2. **EU Directives and Regulations**: Being part of the EU, Malta must comply with various EU directives and regulations that impact real estate practices, including those related to property development, environmental standards, and consumer protection.

Impact of Global Economic and Political Climate

1. **Market Sensitivity to Global Economic Shifts**: The Maltese real estate market is sensitive to global economic

shifts. Economic downturns or instability in key regions can affect foreign investment inflows into Malta's property market.

2. **Political Relations and Diplomacy**: International political relations and diplomacy play a role in Malta's real estate sector. Changes in diplomatic ties or international policies can influence foreign investor sentiment and activity.

Diaspora and Expatriate Communities

1. **Demand from Maltese Diaspora**: There is significant demand for Maltese properties from the Maltese diaspora living abroad, seeking to maintain links with their homeland or invest in vacation homes.

2. **Expatriate Housing Needs**: The presence of a substantial expatriate community in Malta, driven by the thriving iGaming, finance, and technology sectors, influences the residential real estate market, particularly in areas favored by expatriates.

Cultural Exchange and Diverse Architectural Influences

1. **Cultural Exchange and Lifestyles**: International influences contribute to a cultural exchange that impacts lifestyle trends and, consequently, real estate demands. This includes preferences for property styles, amenities, and locations.

2. **Diverse Architectural Influences**: The influx of international investors and designers brings diverse architectural styles and innovations to the Maltese real estate market, enriching the architectural landscape.

Challenges and Opportunities

1. **Balancing Local and Foreign Interests**: One challenge is balancing the interests of local residents with those of

foreign investors, ensuring sustainable and equitable real estate development.

2. **Opportunities for International Collaborations**: The international interest in Maltese real estate opens up opportunities for collaborations with global developers, investors, and real estate professionals, bringing in new expertise and investment.

International perspectives significantly impact the Maltese real estate market, bringing diverse influences, opportunities, and challenges. For investors and property owners in Malta, understanding and adapting to these international factors is crucial for navigating the market effectively. By acknowledging global trends, regulatory environments, and foreign investment dynamics, stakeholders can make informed decisions that capitalize on the unique position of Malta in the global real estate landscape.

12.5: PREPARING FOR THE FUTURE AS A PROPERTY INVESTOR IN MALTA

For property investors in Malta, preparing for the future is about staying ahead of the curve in a dynamic market. This involves not only understanding current market trends but also anticipating future shifts in the real estate landscape. In this section, we explore strategies for future-proofing your property investments in Malta, considering the evolving market conditions, economic factors, and potential changes in the regulatory environment.

Continuous Market Research and Analysis

1. **Stay Informed**: Keeping abreast of market trends, economic indicators, and regulatory changes is essential. Regularly review market reports, attend industry seminars, and network with other professionals to stay informed.

2. **Anticipate Market Shifts**: Understand the factors that drive the Maltese real estate market, including tourism trends, foreign investment flows, and local economic policies. Anticipating these shifts can help you make proactive investment decisions.

Diversification of Investment Portfolio

1. **Spread Risks**: Diversify your investment portfolio across different types of properties (residential, commercial, vacation rentals) and locations within Malta to spread risks.

2. **Explore New Niches**: Be open to investing in emerging niches or areas that show potential for growth. This could include areas slated for development or properties that cater to specific market segments.

Embracing Technological Advancements

1. **Adopt New Technologies**: Leverage technology in property management, marketing, and investment analysis. Utilize property management software, virtual tours, and

data analytics tools to enhance efficiency and decision-making.

2. **Stay Ahead of Tech Trends**: Keep an eye on emerging technologies that could disrupt or enhance the real estate sector, such as blockchain in property transactions or AI in market analysis.

Understanding Regulatory Changes

1. **Compliance with Laws**: Stay updated on changes in property laws, zoning regulations, and tax policies. Compliance with legal requirements is crucial to avoid penalties and safeguard your investments.

2. **Engage with Policy Makers**: Where possible, engage in dialogues with policymakers or participate in forums that discuss potential regulatory changes. This can provide insights into future legal landscapes and their implications for property investment.

Financial Management and Planning

1. **Robust Financial Planning**: Have a solid financial plan in place, including budgeting for maintenance, managing cash flow, and planning for contingencies.

2. **Access to Capital**: Ensure you have access to capital for new investments or to cover unexpected expenses. This may involve maintaining good banking relationships or exploring alternative financing options.

Building and Maintaining Strong Networks

1. **Network with Industry Professionals**: Building relationships with real estate agents, legal advisors, financial experts, and fellow investors can provide valuable insights and opportunities.

2. **Engage with Local Communities**: Understanding and engaging with local communities can offer grassroots

insights into market demands and potential areas of growth or concern.

Focus on Sustainable and Green Investments

1. **Eco-friendly Properties**: Invest in properties with sustainable features or retrofit existing properties to make them more energy-efficient. This not only appeals to environmentally conscious tenants or buyers but can also lead to long-term cost savings.

2. **Stay Informed on Green Regulations**: Monitor developments in environmental regulations and green building standards, as these could impact future property values and marketability.

Adapting to Changing Demographics and Lifestyles

1. **Understand Demographic Shifts**: Malta's changing demographics, including aging populations or shifts in family structures, can impact housing needs. Tailor your investments to cater to these evolving demands.

2. **Lifestyle Trends**: Lifestyle trends, such as the increasing preference for remote work or urban living, can influence the type of properties in demand. Align your investments to cater to these trends.

Risk Assessment and Mitigation

1. **Conduct Regular Risk Assessments**: Regularly assess the risks associated with your property investments, including market volatility, tenant defaults, and natural disasters.

2. **Implement Risk Mitigation Strategies**: Develop strategies to mitigate identified risks. This may involve purchasing adequate insurance coverage, implementing effective property management practices, or maintaining financial reserves.

Long-term Vision and Flexibility

1. **Future-oriented Investment Strategy**: Develop a long-term investment strategy that takes into account potential future market developments and your personal investment goals.

2. **Flexibility to Adapt**: Be prepared to adapt your strategy in response to market changes. Flexibility is key to capitalizing on new opportunities and navigating challenges.

Preparing for the future as a property investor in Malta requires a combination of diligent market research, strategic diversification, embracing technology, and adapting to evolving market conditions. By staying informed, financially prepared, and flexible in your approach, you can position yourself to make the most of the opportunities in Malta's real estate market, while effectively managing potential risks. This proactive and forward-thinking approach is essential for long-term success and sustainability in the ever-changing landscape of property investment.

CONCLUSION

As we draw this comprehensive guide to the Maltese real estate market to a close, it's important to reflect on the journey we've embarked upon together. Throughout this book, we've navigated the intricate layers of Malta's property landscape, unraveling the complexities of market trends, investment strategies, legal frameworks, and the ever-important human element of real estate transactions.

In a market as dynamic and diverse as Malta's, the key takeaway for any investor, seasoned or novice, is the importance of adaptability and informed decision-making. The real estate environment is perpetually evolving, influenced by a myriad of factors including economic shifts, technological advancements, and changing societal norms. As such, maintaining a pulse on these changes and understanding their implications is crucial for success.

Remember, real estate investment is not just about buildings and land; it's deeply rooted in understanding people, communities, and the unique tapestry of the local culture. Whether it's engaging with neighborhood dynamics, anticipating the needs of future tenants, or aligning investment choices with emerging trends, the human-centric approach will continue to be a significant driver of success.

As you move forward in your real estate journey, I encourage you to continue learning, stay curious, and remain open to new opportunities and perspectives. The path to successful property investment is rarely a straight line; it's a journey filled with learning curves, unexpected turns, and invaluable lessons.

I sincerely hope this book has provided you with valuable insights and tools to navigate the Maltese real estate market with confidence and foresight. May your investments be prosperous, your decisions wise, and your experiences enriching.

Finally, I invite you to join me on my blog at www.alistairmcleod.com/blog, where I continue to explore the fascinating world of real estate, share market insights, and delve into the nuances of property investment in Malta and beyond. Your journey in real estate is a continuous learning experience, and I look forward to being a part of it.

Thank you for reading, and I wish you the very best of luck in all your real estate endeavors.

YOUR VOICE MATTERS

A Sincere Thank You and a Call to Share Your Experience

I want to extend my heartfelt gratitude for taking the time to read this guide. Your engagement and interest mean the world to me, and I sincerely hope the information has been valuable in your journey toward property investment and financial freedom. Your feedback is incredibly important; it not only helps me improve but also assists others in finding a resource that can truly make a difference in their lives.

If you found this guide helpful, I kindly ask that you consider leaving an honest review on Amazon. Your insights could be the deciding factor for someone else looking to invest in their financial education.

To leave a review, simply go to "My Orders" on Amazon. Click on 'Write a customer review'. Rate the book and share your thoughts. Every word counts, and your opinion is highly valued.

Thank you once again for your time and trust. Wishing you all the success in your property investment endeavors.

Warm regards,

Alistair McLeod

ABOUT THE AUTHOR

Alistair McLeod is a seasoned real estate expert with over two decades of experience in the global property market. His passion for real estate, combined with his extensive travels, has given him a unique perspective on property acquisition strategies across different cultures and economies. Alistair's dedication to sharing knowledge has made him a sought-after speaker at international seminars and workshops. His writings, characterized by their depth and clarity, have guided countless individuals in their real estate journeys. When he's not penning down insights or advising clients, Alistair enjoys exploring hidden architectural gems around the world.

Visit his website at www.alistairmcleod.com or reach out directly at info@alistairmcleod.com

Printed in Great Britain
by Amazon